Behaving Badly:

Ethical Lessons
from Enron

Denis Collins

First published by Dog Ear Publishing
4010 W. 86th Street, Ste H
Indianapolis, IN 46268
www.dogearpublishing.net

ISBN: 1-59858-160-0
Library of Congress Control Number: 2006928020

This book is printed on acid-free paper.

Printed in the United States of America

Table of Contents

Executive Overview ix

The Author xi

Foreword xii

Introduction...xiv

Part I. REAL-TIME DECISION-MAKING......................1

Chapter 1: The Formation Years

Corporate Raiders: Early 1980s 2
    If you were a Houston Natural Gas executive
    would you...
Ken Lay 5
Another White Knight Opportunity: 1985 7
    If you were Ken Lay would you...
Creating Enron: 1985 to late 1980s 10
Jeff Skilling...11
Salvation through the Gas Bank: 1990 14
    If you were Ken Lay would you...
Enron's New Vision: 1990 and 1991 17
    If you were Ken Lay would you...
Incentivizing Skillingites: Early 1990s.............................20
Andy Fastow: 1990 22

Chapter 2: The Growth Years

Using SPEs to Get Loans Off Enron's
Balance Sheets: 1991 25

Mark-to-Market Accounting: 1991 and 1992 26
    If you were Jeff Skilling would you...
International Expansion: Early 1990 through 1992 30
Cash Flow Problems: 1992 33
SPE Prepay Solutions: 1992 and 1993 35
    If you were a Tier 1 investment banker would
    you...
Bailing Out Rebecca Mark: 1993 and 1994 39
Almost Everyone Is Happy: 1995 and 1996 43
Transferring Managerial Power: 1996 and 1997 45
    If you were Ken Lay would you...
Entering California's Electricity Market: 1996 and 1997 .48
    If you were Michael Kopper would you...
Buying Out CalPERS: 1997 52
Checks and Balances: 1997 54
Conquering Checks and Balances: 1996 and 1997 55
    If you were David Duncan would you...
Year-End Performance and Bailouts:
Fourth Quarter 1997 60
The Turnaround: January through May 1998 61
Funding the World's Transformation with SPEs: 1998 63
Stock Price Success: 1998 and 1999 65
Riding the Bull Market: 1999 67
Buying Help from the LJMs: April through June 1999 68
    If you were an Enron board member would
    you...
Andy Fastow as CFO of the Year: July through September
1999 73
More Complaints about Fastow: October 1999 75
Nigerian Barges for Sale: October through
December 1999 77
    If you were a Merrill Lynch investment banker
    would you...
A $40 Billion Banner Year: December 1999 80
Broadband Rollout: January 2000 81
The Southampton Place Arrangement:
February and March 2000...83

The Raptors: April through July 2000 86
The Stock Price Summit: July and August 2000 89
> If you were an Enron senior executive would
> you…

More Problems and Financial Schemes: September to
December 2000 93
End of the Year Acclaims: December 2000 97

Chapter 3: The Implosion Year

Skilling the CEO: January and February 2001 100
More Public Scrutiny: February and March 2001 103
The Broadband Collapse: March and April 2001 105
> If you were a senior Arthur Andersen partner
> would you…

On Pace to be #1 on the Fortune 500 List: March and April
2001 109
Keeping Up Appearances: May and June 2001 110
> If you were Andy Fastow would you…

Divesting from the LJMs: June and July 2001 115
Skilling Resigns: July and August 2001 116
Lay Learns about Fastow's Raptors: August 2001 119
> If you were Ken Lay would you…

Wall Street Journal Investigation: August 2001 121
> If you were Sherron Watkins would you…

Preparing to Meet with Lay about Fastow's Raptors: August
2001 124
> If you were Sherron Watkins would you…

Meeting with Lay: August 2001 126
> If you were Sherron Watkins would you…

Responding to Watkins: August 2001 128
> If you were Ken Lay would you…

Public Reaction to Fastow's SPEs: August and September
2001 130
Preparing to Announce Third-Quarter Results: September
and October 2001 132
> If you were Ken Lay would you…

Restating Earnings: September and October 2001 135

If you were David Duncan would you...
Andersen's Documentation and Retention Policy: October
2001 137
The Third-Quarter Earnings Announcement:
October 2001 139
    If you were an Enron employee would you...
Media Frenzy: October 2001 142
    If you were Ken Lay would you...
Redundant Documents: October 2001 145
    If you were David Duncan would you...
Fastow's Departure: October 2001 146
    If you were an investment banker would you...
Credit Problems: October 2001 149
Dynegy Merger: October and November 2001 149
    If you were on Dynegy's secret negotiating
    committee would you...
Enron Acquired: November 2001 153
    If you were an Enron investor would you...
The Hero Turned Enemy: November 2001 155
Out of Control: November 2001 157
Bankrupt: November and December 2001 158
    If you were Ken Lay would you...
Waiting for a Phone Call: December 2001
and January 2002 161
Determining Punishments 162
    If you were a federal judge would you...

Part II. WHAT COULD HAVE BEEN DONE
TO MANAGE ETHICAL PERFORMANCE? 167

An Honest Assessment 169
A Moral Compass 171
    Determining Economic Value 173
    Loyalty to an Unethical Boss 176
    Dealing with Unethical Customers 180
    Informing the Public about Financial Problems 183
Seven Moral Levees 185

Acknowledgments 192

References...193

Index 216

A man is incapable of comprehending any argument that interferes with his revenue.

—Rene Descartes

For God did not give us a spirit of timidity, but a spirit of power, and love, and self control.

—2 Timothy 1:7

This book is dedicated to all my former, present, and future students at the University of Wisconsin–Madison, University of Bridgeport, Edgewood College, and elsewhere.

EXECUTIVE OVERVIEW

This book puts the reader in the shoes of Enron executives through the journey of the once prominent and now infamous company, which began as a newly merged firm in 1985 with too much debt, rose on Wall Street during the 1990s, and collapsed in December 2001.

The Enron trial is an indictment of the bullish stock market in the "Roaring 1990s." Democratic capitalism had won the Cold War, entrepreneurs were national heroes, the Internet made business connections across the globe easier, and we would all live happily ever after. Enron stood at the front of the line, brokering natural gas trades that would help reduce what President George W. Bush has referred to as our nation's oil addiction.

What happened? It's easy to paint Ken Lay and Jeff Skilling as villains. But perhaps they are simply a lot like the rest of us. Human beings tend to exaggerate their circumstances, whether they are mid-level managers in a medium-sized company, owners of a small business, or Ken Lay, CEO of the seventh-largest company in the world with annual sales in excess of $100 billion.

Lay and Skilling hid information about poor past performance from shareholders and offered the public positive future scenarios they hoped would come true. There are fine distinctions among the terms "wishful thinking," "exaggeration," and "lying," which philosophers have debated for several thousand years. One thing all three terms hold in common is that the receiver of the information is intentionally deceived.

Lay is considered by many to be the nicest person they ever met and Skilling the brightest person they ever met. Yet, as described in Part I, both executives conspired with other managers to falsify Enron's financial statements.

What can readers do to prevent their companies from becoming another Enron? Enron's sudden collapse in December 2001 was not inevitable, nor did it happen overnight. At any point in time Enron's misdirected evolution could have been corrected. But nobody stepped forward to do so, and the company eventually drowned in a corporate culture flooded with unethical misbehaviors.

In business, our consciences must respond to a unique set of ethical challenges—wealth, competition, and power. We are creatures of habit and, if unprotected by moral levees, our competitive urge to rise to the top of the social hierarchy may result in scandal and bankruptcy.

Long-term growth requires honesty, trust, integrity, and credibility. Organizations with a well-fortified ethical culture have higher degrees of satisfaction and loyalty among employees, customers, suppliers, and investors. These long-term trusting relationships directly benefit the bottom line.

Aspects of Enron's ethical problems can be found in many organizations. How to create and sustain an ethical culture is discussed in Part II. A decision-making tool is provided that can serve as a moral compass. It is applied to four critical decision points to help clarify key issues. Managers can administer the decision-making tool and systematic framework to steer their companies away from the road that Enron traveled.

THE AUTHOR

Denis Collins is Professor of Business at Edgewood College in Madison, Wisconsin, where he teaches classes in management and business ethics and is a Sam M. Walton Free Enterprise Fellow. He holds a Ph.D. in Business Administration from the University of Pittsburgh. Professor Collins has published numerous books and articles in the areas of business ethics, participatory management, organizational change, and service learning. He currently serves on the Editorial Boards of *Encyclopedia of Business Ethics and Society*, *Journal of Business Ethics,* and *Journal of Academic Ethics* and has served on the Board of Governance for the Social Issues in Management Division of the Academy of Management and the International Association for Business and Society.

Three times Professor Collins was voted the outstanding MBA faculty member at the University of Wisconsin–Madison in *Business Week*'s survey of alumni. He was a finalist for the Academy of Management's Distinguished Educator Award. His teachings, writings, and workshops challenge people to practically follow their ideals. He can be reached at dcollins@edgewood.edu, http://business.edgewood.edu/dcollins, and (608) 663-2878.

FOREWORD

Time is short. Everyone is busy. But please take time to read this book. You won't regret it. That is, if you're asking yourself how in God's name could Enron have happened. Or if you wonder if it could happen to your company—or even to you personally. "What!? Me, a Ken Lay or Jeff Skilling or Andy Fastow? You've got to be kidding! I'd not dream of doing those things. I'm ethical, not a crook."

But let Denis Collins show you how easy it is to slide off the ethical pathway and find yourself taking the low road—*without even noticing it!* Most business decisions at Enron were just that—how to grow the company, manage people, keep costs low, make shareholders happy. Nothing much "ethical or unethical" about that—no special advice needed beyond good business judgment. Besides, anyone in doubt could always check the Enron Code of Ethics, one of the best around.

So what went wrong? Follow the story yourself to find out. Collins leads you step by step from the beginning, through the glory days, and to the final crash of one of America's most famous corporations. As the story unfolds, put yourself in the shoes of CEOs Lay and Skilling, CFO Fastow, Arthur Andersen's David Duncan, even whistleblower Sherron Watkins, and all the other actors in this long-running ethics tragedy. *What would you have done? Or done differently? Or more ethically?* That's what Denis Collins asks you to do. Could you—or would you—have made better decisions? Then, take a private moment and honestly ponder your own personal answer. You may wind up being more sympathetic with the Enron bad guys than you first thought.

But the author of *Behaving Badly: Lessons Learned from Enron* offers you a way out of the all-too-human dilemma of facing an ethics crisis at work—one that makes ethics work for the company and everyone involved. You could call it the Denis Collins Business Ethics Toolkit—a simple, logical, ethically sound way of thinking one's way through the kinds of ethics issues that led to Enron's downfall. Don't be put off by its simplicity or ease of use. He has spared you the fuzzy jargon sometimes found in ethics primers. It's the kind of talk used every day in most companies. It's practical. You can put it to work in your own job and company. You'll be glad to have it—and to share it with fellow workers.

Collins himself has had direct hands-on experience in the workplace, so he understands how ethics can look to a decision maker. I guess you could say he's on your side. That's the side the angels are on, isn't it?

William C. Frederick

Professor Emeritus of Business Administration, Katz Graduate School of Business, University of Pittsburgh, and author of *Corporation, Be Good! The Story of Corporate Social Responsibility* and *Values, Nature, and Culture in the American Corporation.*

INTRODUCTION

Enron. The name conjures up images of everything wrong with corporate America. And for good reason. The poster child of the "New Economy" and a darling of Wall Street, Enron's stock price soared through the 1990s, enriching millions of investors. If you bought the stock in August 1999 and sold it one year later, you more than doubled your money. For five consecutive years, Enron won *Fortune* magazine's award for being the nation's most innovative company. In 1999, Enron's chief financial officer Andy Fastow was honored as one of the nation's best CFOs by *CFO Magazine.* One year later, with revenue climbing to $100 billion, *Fortune* named Enron America's best-managed company. In 2000, Enron was ranked #7 on the Fortune 500 list, #22 on the "100 Best Companies to Work for in America" list, #25 on the "Most Admired Company in the World" list, and #31 on the "Fastest Growing Company" list. At the conclusion of the first quarter of 2001, Enron's projected annual revenue was a whopping $240 billion, which would have put Enron in the coveted #1 spot on the Fortune 500 list by the end of the year.

But that is not what happened. Instead, on October 16, 2001, Enron announced a $1 billion write-off and a $1.2 billion accounting mistake. A week later, Fastow was fired, and five weeks after that Enron declared bankruptcy. Enron, the company many hoped would end the nation's addiction to coal and foreign oil by providing clean, domestic natural gas at a reasonable price, imploded.

Enron's demise can be attributed to a wide range of diverse factors, including the personalities of key decision-makers, the organizational culture, economic and political trends, and the nature of capitalism. The same deadly ingredients can destroy any organization if owners and managers are not careful.

In the case of Enron, the fraudulent accounting techniques exposed in late 2001 can be traced back to the early 1990s when Enron adopted aggressive accounting measures for calculating revenue. At the time, the company was trying to financially grow out of the heavy debt incurred following the 1985 merger of the two natural gas pipeline companies that became Enron. Business is first and foremost about increasing wealth, and it was the pursuit of wealth by corporate raiders in the early 1980s that gave birth to Enron and the company's never-ending battle with managing its debt.

PART I

REAL-TIME
DECISION-MAKING

Part I challenges readers to grapple with the real-time decisions faced by Enron executives between 1985 and 2002. Every decision you make defines who you are. Readers step into the shoes of decision-makers during various stages of the Enron scandal and are faced with a simple question: What would you have done if you had been employed at, or doing business with, Enron? The real-life answer appears at the beginning of the ensuing section, on the page following the question. Stop and think about your answer before reading what the real decision-maker decided, and the ramifications that followed.

CHAPTER 1

THE FORMATION YEARS

Corporate Raiders: Early 1980s

In the early 1980s, a corporate raider would quietly purchase large amounts of a company's undervalued stock. He (the raider tended to be male) then publicly announced his intent to buy a controlling interest in the company, creating a demand for the company's stock where none previously existed. The corporate raider railed against what he considered to be a group of incompetent managers and proposed hiring more capable executives for the good of shareholders.

The entrenched managers didn't think themselves incompetent. Wanting to protect their own jobs and careers, they countered with a doomsday takeover scenario in hopes that shareholders would remain loyal to them. Based on rather solid historical evidence, management predicted that the corporate raider would drastically cut costs, selfishly pocket excess cash, transfer the most profitable units to another firm in the raider's stock portfolio, sell other units to the highest bidder, liquidate the remains, and, in the process, disrupt the lives of dedicated employees and community members. Many raiders pursued such strategies because the company's individual parts were worth more than the whole of the organization. Didn't the laws of capitalism dictate maximizing shareholder value, the raiders argued?

Stockholders enjoyed a financial windfall while the corporate raider and managers battled for their hearts, minds, and wallets. The price of the company's previously stagnant stock increased dramatically as more people wanted the premium price the raider would have to pay to obtain a controlling interest in the company. Although the higher stock price made the company a more expensive takeover target, the corporate raider, who already owned a substantial amount of stock, saw the value of his stock portfolio shoot upward.

After management's appeal to shareholders not to sell stock to the raider fell on deaf ears—as was often the case—managers sought a "white knight" willing to buy substantial shares of stock under more friendly conditions. This typically included the continued employment of the current management team. Or, managers could make the company financially unattractive to the corporate raider by either selling off the most highly prized assets or taking on massive debt.

At this point in the poker game, the corporate raider cashed in his chips. The white knight or winning management team would pay the raider a premium stock price, referred to as "greenmail," just to get rid of him. In the end, the raider increased his wealth, which is what it was all really about in the first place. The management team's jobs were once again secure. Unfortunately, the remaining organization was in a financial mess.

This scenario played itself out in the nation's energy industry during the 1980s, which barely survived the 1970s oil crisis and a worldwide recession. Houston, the center of the oil industry, was a mere shell of its previously booming self. Many of its publicly held companies were ready for the pickings by savvy corporate raiders. Houston Natural Gas (HNG), with profits of $123 million on $2 billion in revenue and $3.7 billion in assets, appeared to be the cream of the crop.[1] Oscar Wyatt, an oil and gas baron, set his sights on purchasing HNG to complement another oil company he owned. He declared a willingness to purchase $1.3 billion of HNG stock in 1984. Adding insult to injury, he planned to finance the hostile takeover by borrowing money against HNG's strong credit rating.[2] The battle for control of a good corporate citizen had begun.

> *DECISION CHOICE:* If you were a Houston Natural Gas executive and stockholders ignored your pleas, would you:
>
> *(1) idly watch the corporate raider continue to purchase stock;*
>
> *(2) make the company less financially attractive by selling profitable units or taking on unnecessary debts;*
>
> *(3) seek a "white knight" to purchase the company on friendlier terms;*
>
> *(4) pay the belligerent raider substantial sums of money not to purchase any more company stock; or*
>
> *(5) pursue some other strategy?*
>
> *Why?*

Ken Lay

The managers of HNG deftly averted Wyatt's overtures by borrowing substantial sums of money, which made the company less financially sound. They also called in a few political favors from the state's attorney general, who sued Wyatt. The company eventually made Wyatt go away by paying $42 million for the HNG stock he owned.[3] The company survived Wyatt's bid, but the formerly financially healthy firm now had to manage the unplanned debts it incurred. The board of directors of HNG concluded that the company did indeed need a new CEO. They were very impressed by the president and chief operating officer of a competing Houston-based oil company, who agreed to serve as a white knight if needed; his name was Ken Lay. The board actively recruited Lay and then hired him as HNG's new CEO and chairman of the board.

Becoming CEO was a dream come true for Ken Lay, the ambitious forty-two-year-old son of an ordained Southern Baptist preacher. Born in 1942, Lay grew up in rural poverty as a Missouri farm boy, living without indoor plumbing until the age of eleven. His father financially supported the family with various low-paying jobs—buying and selling chickens, selling door-to-door, and working as a janitor—while spreading the word of God. At the age of twelve, Lay worked full-time during the summer driving farm tractors. The family moved to Columbia, where his older sister attended the University of Missouri on a scholarship to minimize her traveling expenses. Ken also received a university scholarship. The oldest land-grant school west of the Mississippi River fulfilled its mission by providing Lay with an inexpensive higher education that would enable him to move up the economic ladder and make the world a better place.[4]

Lay fulfilled his end of the bargain by studying hard and developing connections with influential people. Lay was very personable and earnest, and he excelled in academics and extracurricular activities despite a stuttering problem. He made a lasting impression on Pinkney Walker, his economics professor. Walker, an ardent proponent of the free market system, inspired Lay to stay in school and earn a master's degree in economics.

After graduating in 1965, Lay became a senior economist and speechwriter for the chief executive of Humble Oil and Refining in Houston. Lay attributed his quick advancement up the economic ladder to his education and enrolled in evening doctoral classes at the University of Houston. He married his college sweetheart the following year. He was of draft age as the Vietnam War heated up, and Lay enlisted in the navy and attended an officer training school. Walker pulled a few political strings and found his protégé an administrative military job at the Pentagon examining the economic impact of withdrawing from the war. Lay leveraged his Pentagon research work into a doctoral degree in economics, which he obtained in 1970.

When Richard Nixon appointed Walker to the Federal Power Commission the following year, Walker hired Lay, who completed his military service in 1971, as his chief aide. Lay quickly made a mark as a deregulation specialist and was promoted to deputy undersecretary of energy in the Department of the Interior. Although he enjoyed the prestige, Lay did not enjoy working in a bureaucratic political environment. Lay's regulatory activities brought him into contact with Jack Bowen, the CEO of Florida Gas. In 1974 Bowen hired Lay as his vice-president of governmental affairs. Bowen and Lay became good friends, and two years later Bowen promoted Lay to president.

Through hard work and the right connections, Lay advanced from a childhood of poverty, when he felt lucky for having lunchmeat to eat on Thanksgiving, to becoming president of a regulated monopoly before the age of forty, with an annual salary of $268,000, equivalent to more than $700,000 in today's money.

Then love, a force more powerful than money or status,

prevented him from becoming the company's CEO. Lay had an affair with his secretary and separated from his wife.[5] Bowen had since become CEO of Transco, a Houston oil company, and was no longer available to protect his protégé from the internal corporate politics his scandalous behavior generated. Nonetheless, Bowen rescued Lay again by offering him a job as Transco's chief operating officer. Lay grabbed the opportunity, which included being groomed to succeed Bowen as CEO of Transco following his anticipated retirement in the late 1980s.

Lay returned to Houston in 1981 with his future wife and her children, and his former wife and their children, just as the price of oil collapsed from $40 to $9 a barrel. He put his abundant energies, knowledge and political skills into saving both his mentor's company and the city he admired. Lay became an industry leader by creating a spot market for the buying and selling of natural gas between producers and consumers. Lay remained at Transco until he impressed HNG's board of directors during Wyatt's unsuccessful hostile takeover attempt. After obtaining Bowen's approval, Lay left Transco to take on the duties as HNG's CEO and chairman in June 1984.

But continuous financial problems in the energy industry attracted more corporate raiders looking to enhance their wealth by purchasing other underperforming corporations. From his CEO perch, Lay's political skills would be needed to fight off a corporate raider going after an energy company operating out of Omaha, Nebraska.

Another White Knight Opportunity: 1985

In 1985, Minneapolis investor Irwin Jacobs, fresh from adding to his fortune by greenmailing the Walt Disney Corporation, set his sights on raiding Omaha's financially troubled InterNorth natural gas company. InterNorth's CEO, wanting to avoid "Irv the Liquidator," contacted Lay about a possible merger with HNG. InterNorth proposed purchasing HNG's $47 stock at $70 a share, for a total price tag of $2.4 billion.[6] A Jacobs takeover would be prevented because, even if he sold off corporate assets, Jacobs could not profitably pay off the merged company's huge debt.

The merger proposal made strategic sense for HNG. The federal government was in the process of deregulating the energy industry, and HNG would jump from being a regional company to a national one, with a network of natural gas pipelines flowing from the East Coast to the West Coast, and from Canada to Mexico. In addition, Lay could multiply his growing personal fortune by cashing in his HNG stock options at the premium price being offered by InterNorth.

But there were some potential negative ramifications for Lay to consider. The combined InterNorth/HNG entity would have a daunting $4.3 billion debt to manage and an anticipated $357 million greenmail payment for the stock Jacobs already owned. This would deplete the firm of badly needed cash.[7] Also, it would be a merger of unequal partners because InterNorth's revenue of $7.5 billion was three times larger than the revenue of HNG. Such a size disparity typically resulted in the smaller firm being taken over by the larger one. Bureaucratic redundancies would have to be eliminated to reduce costs, which would probably mean InterNorth executives gaining control of HNG's assets. Only one CEO would be needed, not two, and corporate control would transfer from Houston to Omaha.

> _DECISION CHOICE._ *If you were Ken Lay would you:*
>
> *(1) reject InterNorth's proposal in order to protect your job, to protect the job of your managers, and to keep Houston Natural Gas headquartered in Houston; or*
>
> *(2) merge with the much larger InterNorth, risk*

many executives losing their jobs due to redun-dancies, cash out your stock options, and begin looking for another CEO position?

Why?

Creating Enron: 1985 to the late 1980s

In May, Lay accepted InterNorth's proposal. But first he worked out a deal to become the merged company's next CEO in two years. He also cashed in $4 million in stock options.[8] Lay immediately impressed a majority of InterNorth/HNG's board of directors with his astute responsiveness to the Reagan Administration's deregulation policies. Lay did not have to wait two years. Just six months later, the InterNorth/HNG CEO lost a major political battle with his board of directors and was fired. The board promoted Lay to CEO, making him the fifth-highest-paid chief executive in the United States.[9]

Merged companies begin with two of everything, and then executives from the two previously independent firms battle for control of the scarce resources. Determining which accounting firm should audit InterNorth/HNG's books was one such battle. Arthur Andersen served as InterNorth's auditor, while HNG employed Deloitte Haskins and Sells. Lay proposed a compromise: hire Deloitte Haskins and Sells for auditing because it was already familiar with InterNorth's larger accounting system, and use Arthur Andersen, a consulting leader in the accounting field, for consulting assignments. The InterNorth-dominated Board disagreed and proposed what they considered a more efficient solution— hire Arthur Andersen for both services. Lay, wanting to develop harmony between himself and the board, changed his mind and agreed with the board's desire.[10]

Lay continued to impress the board of directors and in February 1986 he was given the additional responsibility of being chairman of the board. One of his first major decisions as chairman pertained to a name change. The board agreed on "Enteron," a name recommended by a consulting firm. When the *Wall Street Journal* pointed out that the word's definition meant "intestinal tract," the board of directors held an emergency meeting and dropped the middle letters "te" from the name. The merged entity would be called "Enron."[11]

Enron dug a deep financial hole to avoid Jacobs's hostile takeover attempt. The firm reported losses of $14 million in 1986 and barely avoided defaulting on its debt payments. Credit-rating agencies smelled a corpse and lowered the credit rating for Enron's bonds and commercial paper to "junk" status.[12] Making matters worse, several top oil traders Lay inherited from InterNorth created phony trades with fictitious customers and then fraudulently received millions of dollars in bonuses for the transactions. In addition to altering bank statements, the fraudulent traders wrongly predicted the direction of oil prices, tried to make up for the losses by betting more, and lost again, creating a $1.5 billion problem.[13] Enron was in trouble.

Jeff Skilling

Lay relied heavily on the expertise of external consultants to help him manage Enron's operational problems. Previously, InterNorth used the services of McKinsey and Company, the world's most prestigious consulting firm. McKinsey recruited the brightest MBAs from the nation's most elite universities. Lay depended on McKinsey consultants for pivotal advice on how to integrate InterNorth and HNG's management and computer systems. With the help of McKinsey, Lay convinced Enron's board of directors to situate headquarters in Houston, the center of the energy industry, rather than in Omaha, the home of many board members and InterNorth executives.

Lay wanted Enron to thrive, not merely survive. He understood that the two newly combined organizations needed a common vision to divert themselves from bureaucratic turf battles. He created a new, far-reaching goal to rally the troops: becoming the premier natural gas pipeline in North America. Lay followed his words with actions by offering lucrative salaries and financial bonuses for the best available talent on the market, many of whom did not originally plan on working for a highly regulated energy company in Houston, Texas. Lay was very impressed with the executive potential of one particular McKinsey consultant working on the Enron account—Jeffrey Skilling.

Whereas Lay's "rags-to-riches" story appropriately earned him the Horatio Alger Award, Skilling had always been a master of the universe.[14] Born in 1953, Skilling grew up in an upwardly mobile middle-class family that moved from Pittsburgh to New Jersey to Aurora, Illinois before his teen years. His older brother found him a job doing odds and ends at a fledging community access television station. At age fourteen, Skilling, bored with school, started working there full-time, showing up when school let out at 3:15 p.m. and staying until midnight. He advanced to production director, where he managed people much older than himself. Skilling saved an amazing $15,000—equivalent to $81,000 in today's money—by working long hours at the station during his high school years.[15]

What should a teenager do with all that money? The precocious Skilling invested all of it in the stock market. He bought stock in his father's reliable company at about $8 a share. Fortunately, there was a bull market going on and Skilling watched his stock triple in value to $25 a share, making him richer than most adults he knew. Instead of just letting his stock sit there, he did what many investors do and put the stock to work by using it as collateral for loans to buy other things, such as a new automobile.

Unfortunately, the stock market goes down as well as up, and the bull market transformed into a bear market. The value of Skilling's collateralized stock declined and he now learned all about margin calls. Collateral is liquid, loans are not. Investors have two general options when collateral decreases in value—find more collateral to support the loan or sell the item purchased by the loaned money. Skilling chose to sell his non-collateral stock for cash in an already declining market. The stock declined to $2 a share. Skilling lost his entire stock market investment. He wanted to hold onto the stock until the price went up again, but he kept having to make those margin calls. Despite losing a small fortune, Skilling became hooked on the intellectual excitement of trying to outsmart other stock market investors in predicting a company's future performance.

Skilling's intellectual skills earned him a full scholarship to Southern Methodist University, where he studied engineering. Ill-fated, Skilling experienced a horrible accident while working a summer job between his freshman and sophomore years. Some heavy equipment fell on him, causing severe injuries. The bad news of having to wear a body cast was balanced by the good news of receiving a $3,500 windfall in workmen's compensation. Skilling borrowed against the money to purchase $10,000 in high-risk bonds. He bet that their current high interest rates would soon decline, which would make the bonds a more desired commodity than the stocks. But interest rates continued to rise and, again, he had to liquidate the bonds to pay off his margin calls. For the second time he lost a huge stock market investment, and Skilling was only a college undergraduate. Two weeks later interest rates finally acted as he had predicted. Had he still owned the bonds, he would have made a fortune. Skilling learned that it was good to be a little ahead of the market, but not too far ahead.

Humbled by his need to learn more about how the stock market operated, Skilling switched his major from engineering to business and graduated with a finance degree in 1975. He married his college sweetheart and within two years fast-tracked his way to becoming the youngest executive at First City National Bank in Houston. But corporate life stymied his creativity. Despite an average undergraduate GPA, Skilling verbally dared a regional Harvard University recruiter to reject his MBA admission application. Impressed by Skilling's audacity and free market eloquence, the recruiter offered him a coveted slot in Harvard's program.

Skilling excelled at Harvard, thriving in the school's highly competitive nature. In 1979 the previously grade-challenged Skilling graduated among the top 5 percent of his Harvard MBA class. McKinsey and Company, the prestigious consulting firm, immediately recruited him for their Houston office and focused his skills on the energy industry. Skilling set the record for internal advancement and became McKinsey's youngest partner. People were impressed with his intellectual brilliance, particularly his ability to apply concepts across industries. Skilling could now risk other people's money on his very knowledgeable hunches.

Salvation through the Gas Bank: 1990

In the history of the world, 1989 was a watershed year. East German citizens tore down the Berlin Wall and totalitarian communism collapsed. Democracy had defeated totalitarianism and capitalism had defeated communism. One by one, Soviet satellites declared their independence from Moscow and turned toward the United States, the lone remaining superpower, for economic leadership. President George H. W. Bush spoke about a "new world order." Domestic deregulation policies initiated by President Jimmy Carter in the late 1970s and vigorously pursued by the Reagan Administration during the 1980s would frame global economics. Both Lay and Skilling understood that the world would soon become one transparent global market and the first companies to take advantage of the new political and economic landscapes could jump to the head of the Fortune 500 list.

Lay believed that natural gas—not coal, nuclear power, or oil—was the solution to the nation's energy problems. Coal contributed to global warming, nuclear power led to the Chernobyl disaster, and oil made the nation dependent on Middle East political instability. By the late 1980s, oil accounted for 40 percent of U.S. energy needs, and natural gas—which was cleaner, cheaper, and domestically produced—accounted for

23 percent.[16] Lay and Skilling predicted that natural gas would play a more prominent role in meeting the nation's future energy portfolio, and Enron just happened to own the largest domestic natural gas pipeline.

But similar to the oil market, natural gas producers and users both complained about unpredictable prices. Natural gas prices for 1,000 cubic feet rose in the heavily regulated industry from 50 cents in 1973 to $1.50 in 1977 and to $3 by 1985. Following deregulation in the mid-1980s, prices dropped to under $2 and then sat at around $1.50.[17] Most natural gas users signed thirty-day contracts on the spot market due to these unpredictable price fluctuations. But how could producers and users adequately plan next year's budgets when they had no idea what natural gas prices would be the following month?

Lay and Skilling proved to be a perfect combination for addressing this problem. Lay had been shaping deregulation policies in the energy industry for nearly twenty years and was ready to take a leadership role in the next phase of the industry's evolution, though he was unsure what that would be. Skilling, with a consulting background in banking and asset management, provided the "win-win" answer—a Gas Bank that could reduce economic risks associated with price fluctuations for both producers and users.

Natural gas suppliers could sell their product to Enron through long-term contracts and receive a predictable flow of income. Natural gas users could buy their gas from Enron through long-term contracts at a predictable price. The major obstacle was determining a price appealing to both producers and users that was also very profitable for Enron. The firm would need to employ mathematical wizards, who could accurately predict future natural gas prices, and expert traders who could sell long-term contracts at prices more attractive than what users and producers were getting on the unpredictable spot market.

For instance, instead of a buyer paying $2 for natural gas

on the spot market today and not knowing how much to budget for the next purchase, why not sign a ten-year contract with Enron at a guaranteed $2.50? If prices remained below an average of $2.50 during the next ten years, the buyer would lose because the natural gas could have been purchased at a cheaper price on the spot market. But if the prices averaged more than $2.50 during the next ten years, the buyer could save a substantial amount of money relative to buying on the spot market. As for Enron, it only needed to sell the natural gas at a price that was higher than the purchase price.[18]

But where could Enron obtain the money to buy the natural gas it hoped to sell? Skilling reflected on his high school and college stock market experiences and came up with an idea—leverage Enron's assets. Enron could package the long-term contracts as securities and sell them to investors, similar to how mortgage banks sell investors securities backed by home loans.[19] Enron could also adopt other investment banking–like activities, such as providing natural gas producers with cash up-front for a long-term supply of their product at a discounted price or selling derivatives to minimize losses that could arise out of long-term contractual agreements.

> *DECISION CHOICE. If you were Ken Lay*
> *would you:*
>
> *(1) stay focused on what Enron already excelled*
> *in—distributing natural gas through its own*
> *pipelines; or*
>
> *(2) make a huge investment in creating a Gas*
> *Bank, a very risky financial endeavor never*
> *undertaken before?*
>
> *Why?*

Enron's New Vision: 1990 and 1991

Lay, a longtime advocate of free market economics, jumped at the possibility of reshaping how business was conducted in the natural gas industry. If Skilling's idea worked, public utilities would build more natural gas facilities because the price would be predictable, making the United States less dependent on imported oil or dirty coal.

Lay agreed to create a Gas Bank Division and offered Skilling the opportunity to be the new division's CEO. Skilling could be an entrepreneur within a well-established energy company. The price for taking him away from McKinsey: a $275,000 salary, a $950,000 loan, and a $10 million cash bonus when the division grew to a valuation of $200 million, and $17 million more when the Gas Bank reached a valuation of $400 million.[20] Skilling left McKinsey for Enron in August 1990 to create something that had never been done before.

Lay challenged Richard Kinder, Enron's president and chief operating officer, to implement a new strategic vision for the entire company. Being the *nation's* largest natural gas pipeline was no longer sufficient. Given the victory of global capitalism and Skilling's innovative ideas, Enron was well-situated for international success. The new corporate goal: to become the *world's* largest natural gas company.

Lay and Kinder were classmates at the University of Missouri and considered themselves "Mr. Outside" and "Mr. Inside."[21] Lay marketed Enron to potential customers, lobbied federal and state regulators, and distributed donations to key political decision-makers and causes. Lay helped bring both the 1990 world economic summit and the 1992 Republican National Convention to Houston, donating $250,000 to the latter.[22] Whereas Lay served as Enron's public face, Kinder managed internal operations. Kinder made sure there was enough cash on hand from company operations to pay the bills.

The brick-and-mortar pipeline executives had mixed feelings about Skilling and Enron's expanded mission, concerned that the company might be spreading its resources too thin. Enron's desire for global domination seemed premature given the firm's relatively recent economic problems. As for Skilling, he previously experienced the consultant's luxury of telling others what to do, without the ultimate responsibility for managing the outcome.

But they couldn't argue with success. Shortly after the division's creation, Skilling's Gas Bank generated $800 million in revenue during just one week.[23] In December, a mere four months after taking the job, Skilling struck gold with his first long-term megadeal that would indeed change the nature of the natural gas industry. The New York Power Authority signed a $1.3 billion contract to purchase natural gas over the next twenty-three years at a fixed price of $3.50 per 1,000 cubic feet for the first ten years, compared to the current $1.50 spot market price. After ten years the price would be adjusted based on market rates.[24] The guaranteed fixed price persuaded New York officials to construct a state-of-the-art power station on Long Island. Other states were inspired to do likewise, increasing Enron's customer base.[25] By the end of 1990, Enron's annual revenue rocketed up to $13.2 billion, a 40 percent increase from the previous year.[26]

Ken Lay's turnaround triumph at Enron, along with his well-developed political connections and generous financial contributions to George H. W. Bush's presidential campaign, brought him an offer in late 1991 to replace Texas businessman Robert Mosbacher as the nation's Secretary of Commerce. The United States had successfully invaded Panama to arrest its corrupt political leader General Manuel Noriega and overwhelmingly defeated Iraq in the Gulf War with minimal American casualties. Bush's high approval ratings virtually guaranteed his reelection the following year. Lay could return to Washington, based on the foundation of his company's success, and deregulate the entire business sector.

DECISION CHOICE. If you were Ken Lay trying to reshape the nation's energy and deregulation policies would you:

(1) remain at Enron with its large debts but bright future; or

(2) become Secretary of Commerce?

Why?

Incentivizing Skillingites: Early 1990s

Lay decided to remain at Enron. He preferred the position of Secretary of the Treasury, where he could influence national monetary policy, and he put in a bid for the job if it became available after the 1992 election.[27] In the meantime, as CEO of the nation's largest natural gas company, he could help the nation more by reshaping the energy industry, which had fallen under siege due to the Gulf War. Skilling took on the chore of changing Enron's corporate culture from a conservative good-old-boy system to a highly competitive "survival-of-the-fittest" system. He was surrounded by risk-averse bureaucrats, many with military or engineering backgrounds, who were accustomed to managing in highly regulated markets. He needed more people like Ken Rice, who became a millionaire as a result of the New York Power Authority deal, and he had to hire them before competitors started copying the Gas Bank's business model.

Successful businesspeople often try to reproduce themselves in others. Skilling possessed the same tendency, and he hired people just like himself. Creating new markets required highly innovative people with backgrounds in finance and economics. Skilling used his Harvard connections to attract the brightest students graduating from the nation's elite MBA programs. The "Skillingites" he employed tended to be extremely intelligent, creative, competitive, single-minded MBAs willing to work eighty-hour weeks. Skillingites worked hard and played hard. The playing part came with large expense accounts, including tips for dancers at nearby topless bars.

In exchange for their total commitment to Enron, Skilling provided his new hires the freedom to apply their superior knowledge and skills as they saw fit, and he also offered stock options that would allow them to retire as multimillionaires before they turned forty. Both Lay and Skilling were ardent believers in the power of money to motivate human behavior, having themselves overcome different types of adversity to obtain their current well-paid corporate positions. Skilling dangled lucrative stock options and pay for performance bonuses that matched the top salaries offered at the highest-paying Fortune 500 companies. Reliance on stock options as incentives also had several accounting benefits. Stock options did not appear on a company's profit-and-loss statements and could be deducted as an expense when determining tax liability.

In addition to the lure of stock options, what really attracted this group of go-getters were yearly performance bonuses that could far exceed their annual salary. Skilling offered performance bonuses based on the percentage of the total revenue generated by a deal. Bonus-focused dealmakers were inspired to negotiate a $1 billion contract into a $1.3 billion agreement. The larger the contract, the larger the performance bonus for everyone involved. Word of mouth spread among elite business schools that Skilling's Gas Bank was producing millionaires.

Lay, true to his religious upbringing, understood the importance of balancing an employee's quest for riches with other values. He prominently displayed a set of four core values—Respect, Integrity, Communication, and Excellence (RICE) —in public places. Elevator video screens reminded the fast-paced Skillingites what Enron expected of them:[28]

Respect

We treat others as we would like to be treated ourselves. We do not tolerate abusive or disrespectful treatment. Ruthlessness, callousness and arrogance don't belong here.

Integrity

We work with customers and prospects openly, honestly, and sincerely. When we say we will do something, we will do it; when we say we cannot or will not do something, then we won't do it.

Communication

We have an obligation to communicate. Here, we take the time to talk with one another...and to listen. We believe that information is meant to move and that information moves people.

Excellence

We are satisfied with nothing less than the very best in everything we do. We will continue to raise the bar for everyone. The great fun here will be for all of us to discover just how good we can really be.

Each floor of the twelve-story employee parking garage espoused a different aspiration for drivers to absorb as they drove to the top in search of a parking space: Level 1, Bold; Level 2, Innovative; Level 3, Smart; Level 4, United; Level 5, Ambitious; Level 6, Accomplished; Level 7, Resourceful; Level 8, Creative; Level 9, Confident; Level 10, Adventurous; Level 11, Adaptable; and Level 12, Undaunted.[29] Only those who embodied these values need apply!

One new hire in particular who fulfilled many of these highly desired values was Andy Fastow.

Andy Fastow: 1990

Born in 1961 in suburban New Jersey, Fastow's reputation as a slick wheeler-dealer dated back to his high school days as student council president. A very competitive and self-motivated student, Fastow gave the class valedictory address even though he didn't have the highest grades. He majored in both economics and Chinese at Tufts University in Boston as preparation for China's anticipated economic rise.

Similar to Lay and Skilling, Fastow married his college sweet-heart, but with one major difference—Lea was the heir to a Houston fortune. The Fastows took banking jobs in Chicago. Andy Fastow gravitated toward cutting-edge high finance activities, where his accomplishments included the "1989 Deal of the Year" and contributing $12.8 million to the bank's pretax profits.

Skilling needed someone who could move loans off Enron's balance sheets. In December 1990 he hired Fastow for the Gas Bank's finance group. The Fastows relocated to Houston and settled in at Enron. Andy Fastow quickly became Skilling's confidant. Fastow even named his first son "Jeff" in honor of his new mentor.[30]

People who didn't know Fastow on a working basis considered him quiet and polite. But coworkers and those who did business with him considered Fastow loud, vulgar, obnoxious, and prone to temper tantrums. He shoved people during disagreements and belittled their efforts, once even getting into a fistfight with a taxi driver over a 70-cent fare disagreement.[31] He released tension with endless pranks, such as driving a small remote-control car up the legs of female employees. Fastow fit in well with the boys-will-be-boys culture being developed by Skilling. Quirky behaviors were accepted, and to some degree encouraged, as long as the employee produced the desired financial outcomes, which Fastow excelled in doing.[32]

Fastow shared another important attribute with Lay and Skilling—a propensity for financial risk-taking. Fastow's initial success at Enron came from raising money through securitization sales that shifted economic risks to outside investors. The Gas Bank had been loaning money to natural gas companies to build pipelines and for research exploration. Fastow created a new stream of revenue by bundling these loans together and selling them to a third party at a discounted price, similar to how lottery winners sell their future winnings for discounted cash upfront. These transactions had the dual virtues of removing loans from, and adding revenue to, Enron's balance sheets. Fastow's preferred third-party participant was a Special Purpose Entity (SPE).

CHAPTER 2

THE GROWTH YEARS

Using SPEs to Get Loans Off Enron's Balance Sheets: 1991

Commonly referred to as "off-balance-sheet" arrangements, SPEs protect company assets from risky business projects. These SPEs have a variety of purposes and structures. They gained favor in the 1970s for securitization transactions, Fastow's specialty. Accounting-wise, an SPE is treated as a separate business entity rather than as a subsidiary. A subsidiary is controlled by the parent company and its liabilities appear on the parent company's balance sheets. If the subsidiary fails, then the parent company must pay the creditors. But an SPE is controlled by an independent management team and its liabilities do not appear on the sponsoring company's balance sheets. If the SPE fails, the sponsoring company's assets are legally protected from the SPE's creditors.[33]

For a business to be classified as an SPE rather than as a subsidiary, it must be independent of the company with which it is conducting business. According to accounting standards, SPE status can be declared if the business entity meets two important criteria: (1) an independent owner must maintain at least a 3 percent equity investment that remains at risk at all times, and (2) the independent owner must exercise managerial control of the SPE.[34]

In its most basic form, Enron's Gas Bank could sell its research and development loans for cash to an SPE. The cash would count as revenue for Enron, and the associated loans would shift from Enron's balance sheets to those of the SPE. As a private company, the SPE's financial statements were not required to be audited by an independent party. A wide variety of companies, including airlines and large manufacturers, used SPEs to finance the purchase of other assets, such as an airplane. The SPE would then lease the asset to the sponsoring company.[35]

With some creativity, Fastow constructed SPEs that generated large financial benefits for both Enron and the SPE. He funded SPEs with as much as 97 percent Enron stock, the highest amount legally allowed, thus requiring no cash from Enron. As Enron's stock increased, so did the economic value of the SPE. This made the SPE attractive to outside investors and provided the SPE with funds for additional securitization purchases. Accounting rules prohibited companies from claiming profits and losses from selling shares of its own stock, so an increase in the value of Enron stock funding the SPE could be claimed by only the SPE, not Enron. However, Enron, as part-owner of the SPE, could, and did, claim SPE profits on its balance sheets.

Fastow quickly became one of Skilling's favorite employees.

Mark-to-Market Accounting: 1991 and 1992

By mid-1991, the Gas Bank division signed long-term contracts with more than thirty-five natural gas producers and fifty users, the largest being Florida Power & Light.[36] Skilling knew his division generated tremendous financial value for

Enron. Unfortunately, it didn't look that way to the outsiders he wanted to impress. The Gas Bank had the same problem as all new startups—revenue pouring in was overwhelmed by substantial startup expenses. But Skilling maintained the real culprit was Enron's traditional pipeline accounting system. The manner in which the economic value of his division's current assets was determined misrepresented economic reality. It ignored the guaranteed long-term future revenue streams.

Knowing the current value of a company's assets enables stockholders to make informed investment decisions. According to Skilling, Enron's business landscape changed and so should its accounting techniques. For instance, the first ten years of the twenty-three-year New York Power Authority contract had a guaranteed set price. Even though the income would be received incrementally over ten years, all of the income was guaranteed and should have been reported on the balance sheets reviewed by investors. In addition, Skilling argued, the Gas Bank should be able to claim the economic value of the final thirteen years of the contract using well-accepted pricing models that predicted the expected value of natural gas. If market rates increased more than initially projected, then the real value of the twenty-three-year contract was proportionally higher than initially projected. Skilling believed that the Gas Bank should be able to book the entire value of the contract immediately and adjust its value on a quarterly basis for anticipated profits and losses due to changes in the market.[37]

Skilling looked toward the financial industry for a more reliable accounting method because his Gas Bank division traded energy the way brokerage firms traded capital. Financial institutions calculated the value of their stock portfolios by marking the stock against the current market price rather than the original purchase price. Why shouldn't Enron use the same method for its trading division?

For instance, assume that an investment bank purchased 100 shares of stock in January at $10 a share. Six months later, the stock is selling for $20 on the open market. What should the investment bank's 100 shares of stock be valued at on its July balance sheets? Historical accounting techniques would value the stock at $1,000 (100 x $10, the original January purchase price) because they hadn't yet been sold. Mark-to-market accounting techniques would value the stock asset at $2,000 (100 x $20, the current July selling price), providing a more accurate snapshot understanding. An investor would prefer to know the current value of the firm's stock holdings rather than what the stock holdings were worth six months or six years ago. Skilling maintained that the same logic applied to his Gas Bank. Enron's portfolio of fixed-price energy trading contracts should be booked at present value and reevaluated on a regular basis. If the value went up, Enron could claim the financial difference as income. If the value went down, Enron could declare a loss.[38]

Skilling proposed that Enron ask the Securities and Exchange Commission (SEC) for a special ruling to become the first nonfinancial institution to use "mark-to-market" accounting techniques for calculating the current value of assets. Mark-to-market would allow the Gas Bank to immediately claim anticipated long-term revenue upon signing a natural gas contract, rather than waiting until the revenue was actually received to claim it. The difference would be huge. Whereas traditional accounting might record the $1.3 billion New York Power Authority agreement as $56 million a year for twenty-three consecutive years, mark-to-market accounting would allow Enron to claim a much higher amount of the guaranteed income in the present accounting period, even though it had not been received. According to Skilling, mark-to-market provided investors with a more realistic understanding of his division's economic value. The Gas Bank operated just like an investment bank and should use the same accounting methods.

Nonetheless, the SEC rejected Enron's initial proposal request, in part because trading companies rely on the market system, an external independent source, to determine the value of its assets. Under the Enron system, analysts employed by Enron would be determining the long-term value of assets, making it more prone to abuse. For instance, price curves could be created to support whatever amount of revenue an Enron executive wanted to claim merely by changing an assumption regarding inflation rates. Skilling pointed out that this sort of manipulation could be prevented through auditor oversight, and Enron employed one of the most prestigious auditors in the world, Arthur Andersen.

> *DECISION CHOICE. If you were Jeff Skilling would you:*
>
> *(1) keep the traditional oil-and-gas accounting system; or*
>
> *(2) appeal the SEC rejection and resubmit a proposal for adopting a mark-to-market accounting system for the Gas Bank?*
>
> *Why?*

International Expansion: Early 1990 through 1992

Skilling did not give up. He organized additional support from Arthur Andersen and the board of directors. On January 30, 1992, the SEC approved Enron's use of mark-to-market accounting beginning in the first quarter of 1992.

Wanting to further impress other Enron executives and investors that his trading division was creating even more financial value than previously reported, Skilling informed the SEC that he would retroactively apply mark-to-market accounting for the recently completed 1991 fiscal year, something the SEC had not ruled on.[39] Doing so generated additional revenue for Enron in 1991, but not cash. It also favorably impacted management's revenue-based year-end performance bonuses. Skilling stood to earn a $10 million bonus when his division's valuation reached $200 million.

But Skilling needed to be careful. An abuse of mark-to-market accounting techniques could lead to fraud. Corporate executives, when they file quarterly financial statements, have a legal obligation to provide an honest accounting of costs and revenues. Investors rely on this information to decide whether to buy, hold, or sell a company's stocks and bonds. It would have been fraudulent for Enron executives to claim future profits in the valuation of assets during the present financial quarter if they knew those future profits were not really forthcoming. Shareholders could sue and the SEC would issue harsh penalties if fraud occurred.

With President George H. W. Bush's international new world order taking shape, Enron's International Operations Division rivaled the Gas Bank's growth potential. Business strategists recommend that global expansion begin with entry into a similar culture to minimize misunderstandings. Enron followed this advice and directed resources toward England, where Prime Minister Margaret Thatcher was following Ronald Reagan's deregulation lead. In 1990 John Wing, a Florida Gas executive Lay brought to Enron, struck gold in Teesside, England. Wing negotiated a contract to construct the world's largest cogeneration plant, one that would supply 3 to 4 percent of Great Britain's electricity needs. Even more impressive were the projected $30 million in annual profits and $100 million construction contract to build the estimated $1.3 billion facility in northeastern England.[40]

Wing possessed Skilling's personality and then some. A graduate of West Point as well as the Harvard Business School, the physically intimidating Wing treated employees, suppliers, and customers as though they were grunts under enemy fire in the middle of a combat zone.[41] At Teesside, his management team constructed additional pipelines, made deals with natural gas suppliers and users, arranged $1.3 billion in financing, and built the plant within twenty-nine months.

Wing made sure his team members were financially rewarded for their sacrifices. Lay, who tended to avoid confrontations, was no match for Wing, who insisted that managerial bonuses be large enough to inspire even bigger international deals. Wing negotiated an $11 million ownership stake in the facility for a handful of managers upon the project's completion.[42] Wing's new financial deal raised the performance bonus benchmark for Skilling and others competing to be the wealthiest executives at Enron.

Wing typified senior executive attitudes toward compensation—if you generate income you deserve a piece of the action—a sentiment with which Lay agreed. According to the ancient Chinese philosopher Lao Tzu, "he who knows he has enough is rich." Wing was not rich, he always needed more money.

Already a multimillionaire through an early investment in the Sam Adams beer corporation, Wing negotiated a five-year $300,000 salary for becoming CEO of Enron's new cogeneration division in 1987. More importantly, he negotiated a 5 percent stake in the division and a financial share of all projects. The latter clause resulted in Wing receiving a guaranteed $300,000 bonus every year for twenty years for the three cogeneration plants he had developed in the United States prior to Teesside.[43] When Enron sold half of one cogeneration plant to raise desperately needed cash, Wing earned 10 percent of the $90 million deal plus $400,000 a year for five years for early termination of the contract.[44] This might seem financially extravagant, particularly given Enron's debt-based problems at the time, but Wing kept negotiating bigger and bigger deals that generated bigger and bigger profits.

With Wing leading the way on creating cogeneration facilities, Lay named Wing's protégé, Rebecca Mark, as CEO of Enron's new international division. Mark's family background matched Lay's. She was raised on a rural Missouri farm by devout Baptist parents. Similar to Skilling and Wing, she earned a Harvard MBA. Nicknamed "Mark the Shark" and "Hell in High Heels," she followed her mentor's lead by making large international deals that generated substantial compensation payouts. A very attractive woman known for having had an affair with Wing, Mark frequently exploited her sexuality in the macho world of international development for the sake of making deals.[45]

Mark possessed a missionary's zeal to provide developing nations with the energy required for their industrialization. Under her leadership, Enron became a partner in the engineering design and construction projects these nations needed to enter into the modern world. In 1992, Enron acquired a South American pipeline company to expand operations into the Southern Hemisphere. The international projects received the full support of the Republican presidential administration.

Then the unexpected happened. Lay's friend George H. W. Bush lost the 1992 presidential election to the former Democratic governor of Arkansas, Bill Clinton.

Cash Flow Problems: 1992

Mark's ability to lobby foreign governments actually improved after the Republicans lost control of the White House. There were now a stable of high-level Republicans with international contacts looking for consulting jobs. Enron signed international consulting contracts with former secretary of state James Baker, former secretary of commerce Robert Mosbacher, and Henry Kissinger. Wendy Lee Gramm, a former member of the Commodity Futures Trading Commission and the wife of powerful Republican Senator Phil Gramm, joined Enron's board of directors.[46] These well-known high-profile consultants were now looking after Enron's interests while attending functions hosted by their high-level international contacts.

The political change in Washington also meant shifting some financial contributions to well-connected Democrats. Although he was a staunch Republican, Lay knew that incumbency mattered much more than ideological purity. Enron donated more than $2 million to Democrats during the two Clinton Administrations. The financial contributions paid particular dividends with the Overseas Private Investment Corporation (OPIC), a federal agency that provides loans and insurance for international development projects. Enron would receive more than $2.2 billion from OPIC for more than a dozen international projects.[47]

The combination of steady profits from natural gas pipeline activities, phenomenal growth in the Gas Bank and International divisions, and the use of mark-to-market accounting techniques resulted in record profits for Enron. In the process of surviving its original debt crisis, Enron became the world's largest natural gas company. Lay now promised Wall Street investors a 15 percent annual growth rate, and linked the goal to executive compensation. When this goal was achieved, he and other executives could vest one-third of their stock options.[48]

Internally, Enron faced several major financial hurdles as its debt kept growing. Mark's international expansion entailed tremendous capital investments that would not generate profits for several years. Worse, Skilling's use of mark-to-market accounting techniques actually made it more difficult to achieve new annual revenue targets. Wall Street analysts continually increased revenue expectations for Enron based on the amount of reported revenue. If Enron inflated revenue during the first quarter, then second quarter expectations would be higher than if Enron hadn't inflated revenue the previous quarter. Bigger deals were needed, where even more mark-to-market revenue could be claimed. This created a cash flow problem because a substantial amount of the Gas Bank's reported revenue was projected, not actual. Optimistic reports of future revenues did not provide the cash needed to fund daily operations.

Kinder warned Enron managers to "not start smoking our own dope" and insisted that performance bonuses be linked to meeting cash flow targets rather than revenue targets.[49] But Lay remained focused on Wall Street's emphasis on revenue growth. A growth strategy meant developing more products, marketing more products in more markets, and, of course, employing more people. All of these growth activities required cash expenditures. Pursuing a growth strategy is like raising teenage children who continually develop more expensive habits, including new clothes they quickly outgrow and need to replace. As a result, Enron borrowed more money to fund new revenue-generating activities to meet higher revenue expectations, which in turn increased corporate debt. This was becoming a vicious cycle spinning out of control.

Skilling and Mark both considered the cash crunch to be a short-term problem, calculating that their creative endeavors would generate huge payouts in a few years. But Wall Street's time horizon was one financial quarter at a time. Enron's immediate cash flow problems could damage its credit rating, making it even more costly and difficult to borrow money.

Finding new ways to transform some of the debt into cash revenue would help address this ever-increasing problem. Skilling turned to his protégé, Andy Fastow, to pull him out of the cash hole.

SPE Prepay Solutions: 1992 and 1993

During 1992, Skilling was concerned about Enron's worsening debt-to-equity ratio. Investors tend to avoid firms with high debt-to-equity ratios, preferring to invest in firms that fund their expenses with cash from operations rather than borrowed money. Debt-to-equity ratios also impact a company's credit rating. A lower debt-to-equity ratio meant a better credit rating, lower cost of borrowing, and more capital available for borrowing.

Fastow had a proposal. Since early 1991, he had been reducing Enron's debt-to-equity ratio by selling securitizations to SPEs for cash, which in turn counted as revenue on Enron's balance sheet. Securities were only one type of asset. In the energy industry, SPEs were created to borrow money for oil well exploration. Fastow recommended creating other types of SPEs to help reduce Enron's growing cash flow and debt-to-equity problems.

This raised several possibilities. An SPE funded primarily with Enron stock could borrow money to purchase either an asset for Enron's use, such as more pipelines, or to purchase an asset from Enron, such as an underperforming power plant. Or, an SPE and Enron could jointly own an asset, with Enron recording income from the asset and the SPE recording the debt. The possibilities seemed endless.

The primary risk in doing business with these types of SPEs pertained to the SPE's independent management team making key decisions that might be contrary to Enron's interests. To achieve Enron's desired goals, the interests of the independent managers would have to be strictly aligned with Enron's interests. Fastow designed several win-win strategies between Enron and Enron-sponsored SPEs that significantly aligned potentially competing interests.

If outside investors were promised a high probability for a large return-on-investment, Fastow reasoned, they might be willing to provide the equity needed to create an SPE that could buy power plants for, or from, Enron. Investors, ignorant of power plant operations, would have to rely upon Enron's expertise. Because the SPE would be substantially funded with Enron stock, an increase in Enron's stock price would enhance the value of the SPE's assets and provide leverage to obtain additional funds for other investments.

Beginning in 1992, Fastow created this type of SPE whenever Skilling needed additional revenue to meet quarterly performance targets.[50] The SPE's success depended on recruiting an independent owner who would be compliant with Enron's immediate desires. The most likely candidates were individuals already earning large fees from Enron who had excess cash, such as investment bankers, notably those at Chase Manhattan and Citigroup.[51]

The investment bankers solicited by Fastow expressed two major concerns. First, if the SPE purchased an asset from Enron, where would the asset be physically stored? No problem, Fastow countered, the asset would temporarily remain with Enron until the SPE obtained a legitimate buyer. Accounting-wise, the transaction would be treated as a "prepay" on Enron's financial statements, where a customer pays cash for a product prior to delivery.

Second, what if the purchased asset lost, rather than gained, economic value over time? For instance, what if the SPE purchased natural gas from Enron and its price went down instead of up when owned by the SPE? No problem, Fastow countered, the SPE could resell the asset back to Enron at a guaranteed profit.

However, guaranteeing profits to investors violated a key component of an SPE—the independent owner's investment had to be at risk. Otherwise, the SPE's assets and liabilities would have to be consolidated on Enron's balance sheets, which would defeat the purpose of creating the SPE in the first place. No problem, Fastow again countered, Enron's guarantee to buy back the asset would be verbal, not written. In addition, Arthur Andersen auditors would not be informed about these unwritten side agreements.

When all was said and done, Fastow found a complex way to obtain a loan from an investment banker that could be recorded as cash on Enron's financial statements. This accounting sleight of hand was quite devious. Imagine Kim needing just another $1,000 to make a monthly sales quota that would earn Kim a $200 bonus. Kim can't find any legitimate customers and appeals to Lee, a friend who works for a bank. Lee offers Kim a $1,000 loan to make up for Kim's financial shortfall. But Kim needs a sale, not a loan. Kim then sells Lee a painting for $1,000 cash with the understanding that Kim will buy the painting back early next month for $1,100. Lee, the loan officer, earns $100 on the deal. If Lee had just loaned Kim the money at 5 percent interest, Lee would only have earned $50 interest, so Lee doubles the earnings amount. It cost Kim an extra $50, but because Kim made the monthly sales quota Kim earned a $200 bonus, which more than covers the $100 Kim paid Lee to participate in the transaction. Everyone comes out a winner, as long as the accountants don't find out.[52]

One Enron employee described the general process as follows:

> "Say you have a dog [loan], but you need to create a duck [cash revenue] on the financial statements. Fortunately, there are specific accounting rules for what constitutes a duck: yellow feet, white covering, orange beak. So you take the dog and paint its feet yellow and its fur white and paste an orange plastic beak on its nose, and then you say to your accountants, 'This

is a duck! Don't you agree that it's a duck?' And
the accountants say, 'Yes, according to the rules,
this is a duck.' Everybody knows that it's a dog,
not a duck, but that doesn't matter, because
you've met the rules for calling it a duck."[53]

Fastow ranked investment banks according to Tier 1,
Tier 2, and Tier 3 status, with Tier 1 being the banks that
received the largest fees from doing business with the Gas
Bank. If these banks wanted to retain their Tier 1 status, they
had to participate or they would be dropped down to Tier 3
status when the Gas Bank went looking for additional funding.

> *DECISION CHOICE. If you were a Tier 1 invest-
> ment banker earning large fees from doing busi-
> ness with Enron and Andy Fastow asked you to
> participate in a "prepay" with guaranteed profits
> would you:*
>
> *(1) accept the offer;*
>
> *(2) reject the offer and risk losing future fees from
> Enron; and/or*
>
> *(3) notify Arthur Andersen about these secret side
> agreements?*
>
> *Why?*

Bailing Out Rebecca Mark: 1993 and 1994

It was not too difficult for Fastow to find investment bankers willing to participate in his prepay scheme. Importantly, many SPEs were legitimately buying assets with Enron. In 1993, the California Public Employees' Retirement System (CalPERS), the nation's largest public-sector pension fund, approached Skilling about energy industry investment opportunities.[54] Fastow proposed creating an SPE partnership between the highly respected CalPERS and Enron, called "JEDI"—Fastow was a big *Star Wars* fan—funded with $250 million cash from CalPERS and $250 million worth of Enron stock that could be used as collateral for loans. Then JEDI would invest in energy startup companies and sell them for a profit when their value increased.

Without having borrowed any money, Skilling had someone else's $250 million in cash to invest. CalPERS, on the other hand, benefited from Enron's expert knowledge of energy industry investment opportunities. In addition, CalPERS financially benefited when the Enron stock it owned through JEDI increased in value. If Enron's stock price doubled, CalPERS's $250 million investment in an SPE worth $500 million would now be an investment in an SPE worth $750 million, a much better return on the original investment. CalPERS supported the idea and invested in JEDI, further solidifying Fastow as Skilling's "can-do" person.

Rebecca Mark had to one-up her two major corporate rivals, John Wing and Jeff Skilling. She set her sights on an underdeveloped democracy in desperate need of energy sources to fuel its modernizing efforts—India.

Lay and Skilling found India very appealing for politically idealistic reasons. India had constantly been a thorn in the side of the United States during the Cold War, a democracy that leaned in the direction of the Soviet Union. The United States government was more than willing to help Enron form political and economic relationships within India in hopes of changing its political landscape.

India also appealed to Enron's desire to conquer big challenges. Although just one-fourth its size, India had more than three times the population of the United States and was projected to surpass one billion people by 2000—a potentially huge customer base. Success in India could generate tremendous profits for Enron over the next few decades. Determining how to supply India with sufficient energy for industrialization was an intellectual challenge many Enron employees welcomed.

There were just two major obstacles: a lack of infrastructure—which Enron could help remedy—and political corruption. Political power might not absolutely corrupt, but the opportunities for the politically powerful to engage in corrupt activities are endless. Personal integrity, moral courage, and self-sacrifice are often required to avoid corruption in developing nations. India is typically grouped among the most corrupt nations in the world. Those wanting access to high-level politicians must compete with everyone else wanting access to the same high-level politicians, which often means providing incentives for the political leader's gatekeepers. Mark provided $20 million in "educational" donations that may or may not have found their way into educational budgets.

Mark teamed up with General Electric, Bechtel, and a local utility board in India to create the Dabhol Power Company (DPC). Dabhol, a community of 20,000 people in the state of Maharashtra, is located 150 miles south of Bombay, India's financial capital. The DPC proposed building a $2.9 billion power plant that could provide 20 percent of India's energy needs beginning in 1997. Bechtel would design the plant, General Electric would provide the equipment, and Enron would be in charge of daily operations. Bechtel and General Electric each received a 10 percent ownership stake in DPC and Enron received 65 percent. The remaining 15 percent ownership stake belonged to the Maharashtra State Electricity Board, which would be DPC's sole customer. Everyone thought big. The facility would be not only the world's largest gas-fired power plant but also be the largest foreign investment in India.[55]

The business plan's shortcoming lay in determining how the poverty-stricken country would pay for the natural gas produced. A significant portion of Bombay's 15 million residents slept on sidewalks. Analysts estimated that between 15 to 30 percent of India's electricity was stolen, a bad habit that would have to be delicately addressed to avoid riots. Although readily available energy would attract additional foreign investments, the World Bank refused to finance the Dabhol project because it did not believe the project was economically feasible. The agreement terms being negotiated favored Enron at the expense of India's consumers, who lacked the income to pay for the energy produced, which would potentially result in loan defaults.

Nonetheless, Mark's goal for 1993 was to complete the deal by the end of the year and, to everyone's surprise, by December she had obtained all the required signatures for the first phase of the project. India's government signed a twenty-year contract to pay Enron at least $1.3 billion annually for energy produced by the facility, even if unused.[56] The total contract set a new record for Enron, surpassing that of her mentor's Teesside contract.

The project positively impacted Mark's annual performance bonus, but not Enron's precarious debt-to-equity ratio. The annual $1.3 billion revenue would not start arriving for another two to three years, while more debt would be incurred immediately to pay for the startup costs. Again, Wall Street investors were concerned about Enron's current quarter financial condition, not its anticipated status eight or twelve quarters down the road. Making Enron's financial statements look better in the moment would require another creative effort by Fastow.

Importantly, Fastow had an ally not only in Skilling but

also in Kinder, who as president and COO, was responsible for daily operational decisions. He held corporate executives to specific cash and growth targets and, on occasion, successfully minimized financial excess. To meet quarterly targets, Kinder reduced costs by outsourcing key departments, including internal auditing. Kinder also sold Enron's building and then leased it back.[57]

Kinder and Fastow decided that the best way to turn Mark's debt into cash was to create a new business unit, "Enron Global Power and Pipelines" (EPP), and spinning it off as a separate company half-owned by Enron. EPP could buy power plants and pipelines in developing nations, such as the Dabhol facility. The company raised $225 million from investors through an Initial Public Offering (IPO) of stock. Enron sold assets to EPP and profits from these transactions enabled Enron to meet its 1994 earnings targets.[58]

The biggest stumbling block in creating EPP was one that Fastow had already mastered with his SPE endeavors: how to get Enron's auditors and lawyers to agree that EPP was independent of Enron, while making sure that EPP acted in Enron's interest, even when those interests conflicted with the interests of the other EPP stockholders. If Arthur Andersen auditors and Vinson & Elkins lawyers ruled that EPP was really an Enron subsidiary rather than an independent corporation, Dabhol's debts would have to remain on Enron's balance sheet.

Enron chose interlocking board directorates, a common industry practice, as a reliable way to influence EPP's decisions. Enron's president and COO, Kinder, would serve as EPP's chairman of the board. Rod Gray, a member of Enron's board of directors, would serve as EPP's CEO. As for obtaining approval from its auditors and lawyers, Enron paid $750 million to Arthur Andersen and $1.25 million to Vinson & Elkins to provide consulting advice to ensure that EPP met all the legal requirements of an independent corporation. To ensure EPP's independence from Enron, Arthur Andersen and

Vinson & Elkins recommended that EPP create an oversight committee with three independent directors to monitor all transactions with Enron.

It wasn't long before EPP's president, James Alexander, complained to Lay about the inherent conflicts of interests between EPP and Enron. EPP had been forced to buy Enron's underperforming assets at above market rates, transactions that relied on questionable accounting practices. Lay resorted to heavy-handed tactics for organizational discipline. Several EPP senior managers were instructed to report to Skilling rather than Alexander. His power base diluted, Alexander soon resigned.[59]

When all was said and done, Enron's 1993 record profits of $387 million grew to $520 million in 1995.[60] Its stock price reached a healthy $37 a share as 1995 came to a close. The company significantly expanded operations, including establishing a new trading center in London. Enron readjusted its goal from being the world's largest *natural gas* company to becoming the world's leading *energy* company, a quantum leap from the financially unstable regional natural gas pipeline company of 1985.

Almost Everyone Is Happy: 1995 and 1996

Enron's creative accounting techniques made their way into local offices around the globe. Jeff McMahon, the treasurer of British operations, interpreted a new Statement of Financial Accounting Standard to claim up to twenty years of projected profits on power plant hard assets all in one year. McMahon also convinced banks to loan money against future cash flow, which was then miraculously transformed into cash from operations.[61]

Anyone with an Enron business connection seemed to be getting rich. External auditors and lawyers earned millions in consulting fees. Board members received lucrative consulting contracts and cashed in their stock options. In 1993, board member John Urquhart earned a million dollars when he sold phantom equity in one of Enron's units. The following year he received $596,354 in consulting fees from Enron and cashed in $931,000 of stock options.[62]

By far, the happiest person was Ken Lay. He networked with world leaders and played the role of natural gas ambassador both domestically and nationally. He owned more than 3 million shares of Enron stock, up from 300,000 back in 1990, and his stock options were worth tens of millions of dollars.[63] Having sacrificed his time building Enron, Lay felt entitled to the many perks available to top executives. He borrowed money from the company and his family members used the corporate jet for personal reasons. Lay conducted business with his son's firm, then hired him as a vice-president.[64] Enron's lucrative travel business, which generated $2.5 million in commissions, was given to a travel agency owned 50 percent by his sister.[65]

Lay was now a very public figure. He supported a host of charities and had become a Republican Party leader in the local business community. Enron donated millions to politicians and community causes. Lay sat on corporate boards and won awards for being a visionary businessperson and community leader. After Houston's professional football team relocated to Tennessee, he worked to keep the city's professional baseball team. Lay solicited corporate subsidies, and led the effort to pass a 1996 voting referendum to finance a new $265 million professional baseball stadium. Enron paid $100 million to have the stadium named "Enron Field" for a term of thirty years. In return, Enron received a thirty-year contract to manage the stadium's energy needs, worth an estimated $200 million.[66]

The only one not fully happy was the chief architect of Enron's success—Skilling. His increased wealth came at the expense of his health and family. He was overweight, depressed, and having marital problems. Skilling requested a reduction to part-time work status for the sake of his children and marriage. Kinder eventually agreed to an extraordinary job-share arrangement between Skilling and another executive. Under doctor's orders, Skilling lost fifty pounds.[67] But just before the arrangement was implemented, Skilling's job share partner accepted the presidency of another corporation. Skilling's response was to maintain his full-time status with a renewed dedication to Enron, which would contribute, eventually, to a divorce.[68]

Transferring Managerial Power: 1996 and 1997

Lay, having accomplished many of his personal goals, was ready to fulfill his 1992 promise and promote Kinder to CEO by 1997. Under Kinder's leadership, revenue and profits had nearly tripled from 1990 to 1996, while the number of employees increased by only 7 percent, from 7,000 to 7,500.[69] In 1996, Enron was named "America's Most Innovative Company" by *Fortune* magazine and its stock price rose 15 percent, ending the year at $43 a share.

Kinder's only blemish was being three percentage points short of Enron's 15 percent earnings growth target, a shortcoming attributed to Skilling's traders betting wrong on the price of gas. Acquiring a company for $95 million and reevaluating it a few months later at $140 million, with Arthur Andersen's permission, minimized the damage.[70] Kinder was the perfect "Mr. Inside" to Lay's "Mr. Outside." But then Kinder made an internal political mistake of grand proportions.

Extramarital affairs involving Enron executives were not out of the ordinary, and it was well known that Lay's second wife was his former secretary. Kinder's transgression was having an office affair with the wrong person—his boss's secretary. Kinder's secret affair with Lay's secretary made Kinder privy to confidential information, violating a bond of corporate trust.[71] Lay asked for, and received, Kinder's resignation. Lay, who had wanted to move on, had to stay as CEO and also temporarily take on Kinder's COO and president duties. In presenting the turn of events to the media, Lay falsely claimed that he decided to remain as CEO, forcing Kinder's decision to resign.[72]

Kinder left with a golden parachute: $2.5 million in cash, forgiveness of a $4 million company loan, and $109,472 in unused vacation pay. He sold $40 million in Enron stock, which he used to purchase Enron Liquids Pipeline from the company, of which he made himself CEO.[73] As for Lay, he signed another five-year contract to be both CEO and chairman of the board, received an additional million stock options, and started searching for a new COO.

Lay now had to make one of his most important decisions. Should the new COO come from the traditional brick-and-mortar pipeline division, the new natural gas trading division, the booming international division, or should he look for an outsider? Each option could set a different trajectory for the organization.

Skilling was considered the frontrunner since his division now accounted for 20 percent of Enron's total earnings. However, several weaknesses needed to be considered. He was an entrepreneurial visionary who excelled in strategy like Lay, not a hands-on cash manager like Kinder. Kinder and Lay performed well as a team because they were complementary, whereas Skilling was simply a much harsher version of Lay. Also, Skilling took major gambles and it isn't wise for a gambler to be put in control of budgeting. In addition, Skilling lacked patience for those who did not quickly pick up on his intellectual insights. Skilling didn't want to hear about managerial problems, he only wanted to hear about managerial solutions to problems. These attributes are better suited for a CEO than a COO managing the daily details of a business.

Skilling knew this. He also knew being COO was a stepping stone for succeeding Lay as CEO. As COO, and later

CEO of Enron, Skilling would have the opportunity to transform the entire American business system based on his "new economy" model. His recently signed contract stipulated that he would receive a $1 million payout if not granted a promotion by February 1997.[74] Ever the skilled negotiator, Skilling threatened to quit if Mark was promoted to COO.[75]

Although Mark had obtained significant contracts in India and elsewhere, Skilling and Mark, highly competitive Harvard MBAs, did not get along. They often criticized each other in public. Mark accused Skilling of unethical dealings with others, manipulating financial numbers, and being disrespectful of anyone outside his own clique.[76] Skilling accused Mark of mismanaging the international division, creating a huge financial black hole. She would make splashy deals, he claimed, by exaggerating demand and earning huge bonuses. But, in the end, the results were not profitable. Whereas Skilling's operating profits had risen 78 percent, Mark's operating profits had risen by only 7 percent.[77] Skilling strongly advocated for the position, maintaining that the new economy valued intellectual skills and market transactions more highly than brick-and-mortar assets. Only he possessed the appropriate vision for Enron's role in the new economy.

> *DECISION CHOICE. If you were Ken Lay who would you promote to COO:*
>
> *(1) Jeff Skilling,*
>
> *(2) Rebecca Mark,*
>
> *(3) a brick-and-mortar pipeline division executive, or*
>
> *(4) a highly qualified outsider?*
>
> *Why?*

Entering California's Electricity Market: 1996 and 1997

Lay opted for Skilling, who took on the duties of COO in March 1997. Skilling quickly began planning to succeed Lay as CEO. To avoid any second-guessing by Lay, Skilling's contract contained a clause entitling him to $20 million if he was not named CEO by the end of 2000.[78] Lay directed Skilling to repair his relationships with other division executives. Enron's point of view needed to be broader than that of the Gas Bank.

With his power extended to other divisions, Skilling inserted loyalists in key executive positions throughout the company. He promoted Fastow to vice-president of Treasury and Business Funding, with a goal of raising $20 billion a year in capital.[79] Everyone at Enron who needed capital would have to cooperate with Fastow's group. If they didn't, Fastow reminded them, he could ruin their careers.

Fastow convinced Skilling to change the finance department's mission from that of a "cost center" that supported other functions to a "profit center" that generated revenue.[80] Skilling's marching orders for his lieutenants was to make up for Enron's missed earnings target in 1996, which meant impressing Wall Street investors with revenue growth. If anyone needed financial help, they were directed to Fastow.

Skilling had four years to make his case for CEO. He challenged his executive staff to apply the successful Gas Bank business model to other operational areas. The plan was simple: find an untapped area of business, buy some assets, don't worry about initial costs, and get the revenue numbers up. Soon, sales volume would more than make up for sunk costs.[81] Skilling went on a buying spree, purchasing assets in other industries—such as paper and coal—and creating ways to trade key commodities between potential buyers and sellers, with Enron getting a small percentage of each transaction.

Skilling began with electricity, an industry that had many similarities to the natural gas industry. The electricity industry had been undergoing deregulation since 1992, with the passage of the federal Energy Policy Act. Electricity was a $91 billion market, three times larger than the natural gas market. Skilling set a goal to capture 20 percent of the market share, which would translate into an additional $18 billion in revenue for Enron.[82]

Lay and Skilling surveyed the electric utility landscape, setting their sights on California as the state with the greatest potential for developing market-based alternatives to public monopolies. Enron already had a presence there, owning several wind farms that received government subsidies for providing an alternative source of energy. California, a bellwether state whose innovative public policy experiments were often adopted by other states, was already holding public hearings on deregulating electricity. The Harvard Electricity Policy Group, funded by Enron, proposed modifying Skilling's Gas Bank model for California's electricity market.[83] As soon as California governor Pete Wilson signed the deregulation legislation in 1996, Enron purchased Portland General Electric for $3 billion, a 46 percent stock premium. Portland General Electric not only serviced Oregon, but also, as California's northern neighbor, had access to California's power grid.[84]

The purchase of Portland General Electric made Enron an electricity holding company. Unfortunately, a federal law precluded alternative energy companies that were more than 50 percent owned by electric companies from receiving government subsidies. This meant Enron's wind farms would lose their government subsidy at a time when Enron needed more, not less, revenue.

Enron already had a $142 million negative cash flow for the first quarter of 1997, and projections for the second quarter suggested negative cash flow would double or triple. [85] Unexpected price fluctuations at Teesside had cost Enron $1.5 billion. Enron also anticipated lawsuits from the families of thirty-three people who were killed when a San Juan natural gas pipeline exploded from gas leaks that Enron had known about.[86] In addition, the Dabhol facility that should have begun creating operating revenue in 1997 wasn't close to being built yet. The ruling political party in India that signed Mark's lucrative contracts had been voted out of office, and the new government administration demanded a much more favorable renegotiation. Enron's stock price was stuck at $40 a share and the company's cash flow would only worsen if Enron lost its wind farm subsidies, further damaging investor confidence.

What to do?

Fastow, who had successfully funded Skilling's growth strategy for the Gas Bank division, took on the assignment of finding a win-win-win strategy, in which Enron could own Portland General Electric, maintain government subsidies for its wind farms, and improve cash flow. The solution, by now, was standard operating procedure: create an independent SPE, 97 percent funded by Enron, to purchase a majority of Enron's investment in wind farms.[87] The SPE, called "RADR," borrowed money to pay Enron $17 million cash for an ownership stake in the wind farms, which removed the wind farms' debt from Enron's balance sheets. Enron could claim RADR's profits because Enron continued to maintain a large minority stake in the wind farms.

Outside investors profited quite nicely in Fastow-structured SPEs. Fastow now wanted some of the economic rewards generated by his creative financial work for himself. Instead of lining up the usual investment banks to pay for the SPE's required independent 3 percent equity stake, Fastow wanted to personally provide the required $510,000 so he could profit from the investment. However, Enron's Code of Ethics prohibited senior executives from having a financial stake in any organization doing business with Enron. Otherwise, a conflict of interest could arise, compromising an executive's legal obligation to provide honest services to Enron and its shareholders: would the senior executive/investor represent Enron, trying to sell an asset to RADR for the highest possible price, or represent RADR, trying to buy an asset from Enron at the lowest possible price?[88] Enron's Code of Ethics prevented this conflict of interest from occurring.

Yet Fastow wanted a piece of the action. He approached Michael Kopper, his assistant and protégé, with a scheme that would take advantage of a potential loophole in Enron's Code of Ethics. Kopper could serve as the SPE's outside partner because Enron's Code of Ethics mentioned only senior executives in its prohibitions, not their assistants or any other employee. Fastow could loan Kopper the money, and Kopper, in turn, could pay him back from profits generated by RADR's deals with Enron.

> *DECISION CHOICE. If you were Michael Kopper and your boss, a senior executive, requested that you invest in an organization conducting business with your company would you:*
>
> *(1) support the plan,*
>
> *(2) risk getting fired for refusing to participate,*
>
> *(3) inform the CEO about the scheme,*
>
> *(4) notify the auditors about the scheme, and/or*
>
> *(5) notify the SEC about the scheme?*
>
> *Why?*

Buying Out CalPERS: 1997

Fastow and Kopper thought better of the scheme, fearing that the link to Fastow would be too obvious. Fastow finessed further, looking to add another layer or two of economic relationships to obscure his personal involvement. In May, Lea Fastow, his wife, loaned Kopper $419,000. Kopper funneled the money to a group referred to as "Friends of Enron," which then invested in RADR as independent outsiders. The primary investor in "Friends of Enron" was Kopper's domestic partner, Bill Dodson.[89] In August, Fastow distributed $481,850 in RADR proceeds to Kopper, a $63,000 profit in just three months. Kopper funneled the money back to Fastow by writing "gift" checks to Lea, Andy, and the Fastow children that were below the minimum amount required to be reported to the IRS for tax purposes.

This network of relationships, hidden from sight, violated both accounting principles and company policy. The SPE was not being managed by an independent partner, which violated accounting principles. Dodson's name might have appeared on the legal documents, but Fastow was the actual manager. He received compensation for his efforts, a clear violation of company policy.[90] Fastow kept Arthur Andersen ignorant of both violations.

Fastow envisioned other ways for RADR to financially benefit both Enron and himself. But to implement these ideas, RADR needed real outside investors. He approached CalPERS, which had already profited handsomely from its JEDI investment and saw even bigger earnings opportunities, under the assumption that CalPERS's involvement would attract other investors. CalPERS agreed to invest in RADR, but only if either Enron or another third party bought CalPERS's investment in JEDI, which had grown in value from $250 million to $383 million during the past four years. CalPERS gave Enron a November 6 deadline to come up with a buyer.[91] If Enron bought out CalPERS, JEDI's $1 billion debt would end up on its balance sheet, so that possibility was ruled out. Skilling and Fastow agreed that a third party needed to be found to buy CalPERS's $383 million JEDI investment.

Fastow created a special projects team within the finance department, led by Kopper, to work out the arrangement. In November, with the deadline approaching, the special projects team created an SPE called "Chewco," which would purchase CalPERS's investment in JEDI. The $383 million Chewco needed would consist of a Fastow-arranged $132 million loan from Enron, a $240 million loan from Barclay's Bank guaranteed by Enron, and $11 million from an outside investor needed to fulfill the legal 3 percent requirement for an SPE. Fastow proposed that his wife's family provide the $11 million in financing, and that he would manage Chewco's investments. Fastow requested an exemption from the Code of Ethics that would allow him to serve as Chewco's manager. Skilling and Enron's lawyers objected, claiming that the arrangement would still violate the laws governing SPEs that required an independent investor and manager.[92]

Fastow once again requested that Kopper serve as his proxy. But Kopper did not have $11 million to invest. Kopper and his domestic partner Dodson were able to raise $125,000, with the understanding that they would immediately receive $140,000 in management fees. They then worked out a complicated deal with Fastow to borrow the remaining money.[93] Fastow created two other SPEs, which Kopper would manage, that could borrow the remaining money from Barclay's Bank through a loan guaranteed by Enron. Unknown to Arthur Andersen, Fastow made side agreements with Barclay that protected the bank's investment.[94]

More than 99 percent of Chewco's investment was, ultimately, linked with Enron. As a result, Chewco did not meet the legal requirements for receiving the SPE accounting treatment. But Fastow believed there were enough layers of SPEs between Chewco and Enron that no one would notice. Everyone at Enron was working long hours and had other things to worry about. Fastow named Kopper Chewco's managing director. He gave his wife Lea an administrative position with an annual salary of $54,000, although she mostly stayed at home with the kids. Chewco's purchase of JEDI was recorded as cash generated from Enron's operations.[95]

Checks and Balances: 1997

Even though Enron was a relatively flat organization, there were at least six layers of checks and balances to ensure that minimally supervised Skillingites working on SPE activities appropriately pursued Enron's financial interests when these were in conflict with their own financial interests.

First, Enron's risk assessment and control (RAC) department calculated the economic impact of deals being proposed by traders, international power plant developers, and Fastow's growing legion of assistants. RAC personnel focused solely on a deal's impact on Enron's bottom line, not its impact on an SPE or an employee's performance bonus.

Second, the human resources department utilized state-of-the-art, 360-degree performance evaluations that included confidential feedback not only from an employee's supervisor, but also from her subordinates, peers, and colleagues working in other departments.

Third, Enron employees selling assets to SPEs were held accountable to Enron-based performance measures.

Fourth, outside lawyers provided legal advice on the creation of SPEs. Vinson & Elkins, Houston's preeminent law firm, whose partners had close relationships with the federal government, earned significant fees verifying that all structures and transactions met legal requirements. Lawyers were held accountable to their own professional code of conduct, which, if violated, could result in losing their license to practice law.

Fifth, outside auditors ensured that all transactions met Generally Accepted Accounting Principles (GAAP). Arthur

Andersen, Enron's longtime auditor and the nation's largest accounting firm, was well respected for its ethical heritage. Auditors were also held accountable to their own professional code of conduct, which, if violated, could result in losing their license to practice accounting.

Sixth, Enron's board of directors, composed of high-level executives with specialized industry knowledge, had final authority to approve or disapprove of all transactions. Stockholders entrusted board members to ensure honest services by all corporate employees.

In order to enrich himself through the SPEs, Fastow would have to create ways to overcome each check and balance.

Conquering Checks and Balances: 1996 and 1997

Fastow's previously created SPEs—approved by outside lawyers, auditors, and board members—enriched Enron. Chewco and RADR, on the other hand, were structured to enrich Fastow as well as Enron—and sometimes at Enron's expense. Despite the layered checks and balances, Fastow anticipated only minimal objections from the oversight mechanisms, even though the web of SPEs supporting Chewco had expanded into the realms of illegality. The relationships among the SPEs and Enron had become so complex, and Fastow's presentations about them so misleading, that only an auditor dedicated to finding a known fraud in the web of relationships would be able to unravel the illegality.

Oversight by internal and external watchdogs was also clouded by conflicting financial interests and outright manipulation. Any individual effort to stop Fastow was equivalent to jumping in front of a speeding train overflowing with celebrants. As a result, individuals at each level of checks and balances assumed that if the SPE arrangements were questionable or illegal, they would be caught at the next level of checks and balances. But no one had the moral courage to challenge Fastow. As a result, Fastow, for the most part, went unchallenged. Those holding authority at each successive level assumed that Fastow's deals were legitimate because the previous level hadn't objected.

Skilling and Fastow achieved compliance from RAC members and other internal watchdogs by manipulating Enron's semiannual performance evaluation process. In the early 1990s, Rich Kinder closely monitored labor costs by putting hiring limits on Skilling, then CEO of the expanding Gas Bank division. Skilling, wanting to employ more aggressive MBAs, circumvented this limitation by implementing a "survival of the fittest" performance appraisal system. He created a Performance Review Committee (PRC) composed of loyalists who evaluated every employee on a scale of one through five (best to worst) twice a year. Input included 360-degree performance evaluations and other performance-based measures. A specified percentage of employees were assigned each rating number. The 10 to 15 percent assigned the dreaded five rating were dismissed. Employees receiving a four rating were put on notice that, absent performance improvements, they would probably be given a five rating at their next review six months later because those dismissed would soon be replaced by new Skillingites competing for ones.[96]

The PRC appraisal process was made company-wide when Skilling became COO. Traders and Fastow's finance group members threatened to rate an RAC employee a five if she or he did not approve their deals. Loyal Skillingites dominated the performance review evaluation process; one negative evaluation submitted by a Skillingite could undo a host of favorable comments submitted by other employees. Fastow's SPEs enabled enough business units to meet their performance goals that a solid network of Enron employees were guaranteed to vote as Fastow requested on performance review cases.

Outside lawyers and auditors were simply co-opted. Work on the Enron account and some SPE deals could generate substantial fees and consulting revenue for lawyers and accountants. Enron was among both Vinson & Elkins and Arthur Andersen's largest clients, vital to each firm's strategic growth plans and profits. Fastow told lawyers and auditors what he wanted to accomplish, and paid them to apply the appropriate laws and rules to achieve his goals. Vinson & Elkins lawyers, who defined their roles as advocating on their client's behalf, developed the supporting legal documentation. Arthur Andersen auditors helped to construct transactions that did not technically violate the GAAP. They empowered Fastow to find new ways to declare revenue and dispose of debt.

Outside investors considered Arthur Andersen to be Enron's most important watchdog. For Andersen, the Enron account had become a "cash cow," a business unit that could be continually milked for additional revenue. More than one hundred Arthur Andersen employees charged billable hours to the Enron audit. Some auditors received perks such as luxurious office space in Enron's corporate offices, automobiles, and downtown Houston lofts.[97] Assignment to the Enron "engagement team" was akin to interviewing for a higher-paying corporate job. Enron hired more than eighty accountants away from Andersen. When Ben Glisan left Arthur Andersen for Enron in 1996, he received a salary increase from $66,000 to $100,000, along with a $15,000 signing bonus and stock options.[98]

The revolving door between Arthur Andersen and Enron meant that Arthur Andersen auditors were sometimes reviewing the accounting work of a former boss or colleague, individuals whose integrity was assumed. Arthur Andersen rotated lead auditors every seven years. In early 1997, David Duncan, a relatively young partner at thirty-eight years old, became Andersen's lead auditor on the Enron account. Duncan had worked with Richard (Rick) Causey on one of Fastow's first SPEs in 1991. Causey had since left Andersen for

Enron and was now Enron's chief accounting officer, the person whose work Duncan would be reviewing.[99]

At Andersen, Duncan had earned a reputation for being a strong client advocate, someone who helped the client achieve desired accounting objectives. He and Causey developed a friendship and they socialized together. Duncan's annual bonus and advancement within Arthur Andersen depended on increasing client fees by 20 percent. Critically questioning Enron's accounting transactions and financial arrangements would mean career suicide, something Fastow and Skilling pointed out to Duncan and his subordinates.[100] If Duncan lost the Enron account his career at Andersen would end. Andersen auditors signed off on some questionable transactions under the assumption that they had been approved by the outside lawyers or, if really questionable, that they would be vetoed by Enron's board of directors.

The cycle of false assumptions was completed at the board level. Board members owned significant shares of Enron stock, earned consulting fees working on Enron projects, and had formed close personal relationships with Ken Lay. The board of directors signed off on questionable transactions under the assumption that the transaction had been previously approved by Andersen auditors, outside lawyers from Vinson & Elkins, and Enron's own RAC department.

The intricate web of win-win relationships was held together by the allure of financial rewards and promotions. At Enron, raises and promotions depended on approval of Fastow and Causey's creative financial schemes and accounting techniques. Arthur Andersen, Vinson & Elkins, and investment banks provided raises and promotions to employees who increased business fees from Enron, which meant pleasing Fastow. Even investors, whose interests the auditors, lawyers, and board of directors oversaw, were winning as Enron's stock price rose steadily.

Fastow's creative SPE schemes saved Enron's fourth-quarter 1997 financial performance. Cash flow went from a negative $588 million at the end of September to a positive $501 million at the end of December, a $1 billion tidal change for a company not dependent on Christmas sales.[101] Some Andersen accountants, led by Carl Bass, objected to Enron's accounting methods. Bass had been working on the Enron account for two years and had developed a low regard for both Fastow and Causey.[102] But Duncan, as the lead engagement partner, had the final say in the matter.

> *DECISION CHOICE. If you were David Duncan, the engagement partner on the Enron account, would you:*
>
> *(1) risk losing the Enron account, which is the basis for your career path within Andersen, by demanding that Fastow and Causey follow more rigorous accounting standards; or*
>
> *(2) risk your professional license by allowing Fastow and Causey to continually manipulate accounting standards?*
>
> *Why?*

Year-End Performance and Bailouts: Fourth Quarter 1997

Duncan consistently supported Causey and Fastow's interpretation of accounting rules. Bass determined that Enron had inappropriately booked income, but Duncan overruled him, allowing Enron to nearly double its annual profits from $54 million to $105 million.[103]

Fraudulent accounting for SPE transactions resulted in additional net income of $28 million, reduced debt by $711 million, and made Enron more attractive to outside investors.[104] Taking into consideration all the accounting mistakes, Enron's profits for 1997 should have been only $8 million, not the $105 million that was reported.[105]

Even with such drastic accounting manipulation, Enron's financial performance under Skilling paled in comparison to Kinder, his predecessor. In 1996, under Kinder, Enron achieved $584 million of profits on $13 billion revenue; Enron's reported $105 million of profits on $20 billion revenue in 1997 under Skilling represented the company's lowest profit total in nearly a decade.[106]

What went wrong? Expenses skyrocketed. Capital expenditures and long-term debt both doubled, resulting in a 44 percent increase in interest expenses.[107] The number of employees also doubled in one year, from 7,500 to 15,000, way out of line with previous labor cost projections. Enron's traders, who now accounted for one-third of all employees, continued to earn huge bonuses, fly first-class, drive limos to luxury hotels, and submit $10,000 expense reports, including $2 million for flowers.[108] Enron owned several corporate jets, and Lay's $300,000 bill for airplane use was petty cash compared to Rebecca Mark's $6 million airplane budget.[109] Managerial stock options ballooned from twenty-five to thirty-nine million shares and year-end bonuses included $1.7 million for Fastow, $2 million for Skilling, and $3.6 million for Lay.[110]

Enron's stock dropped from $43.10 at the end of 1996 to $41.60 at the end of 1997. Skilling interpreted this as a vote of no confidence from investors since the Standard & Poor's 500 Index had increased 31 percent during his first year as COO.[111] The stock market took off without Enron. Skilling pledged this would not happen again.

The Turnaround: January through May 1998

Enron's stock price fell further with the start of the new year, to $38.50 a share on January 8. Skilling and other executives more vigorously wined and dined Wall Street analysts to gain their support for the new markets being developed by Enron, such as selling weather derivatives to ensure income when extreme weather conditions negatively impacted a company's operations. Selling derivatives was particularly appealing because, in 1996, the Financial Accounting Standards Board extended the use of mark-to-market accounting techniques to all financial derivatives. Skilling also heavily funded Enron Energy Services (EES) to sell energy directly to homes and businesses rather than public utilities. In an act of audacity that would become Enron folklore, Skilling hosted several dozen Wall Street analysts who toured EES's hectic trading-floor activities. What appeared to be busy salespeople finalizing telephone deals with customers actually consisted of secretaries, sitting in front of nonfunctioning computers, telephoning friends.[112]

Tragedy almost struck Enron when a member of Fastow's department prematurely shared Enron's latest financial numbers with creditors, prior to the completion of the accounting manipulations. The submitted information revealed that Enron did not have enough cash to cover its interest payments. Moody's credit-rating agency gave Fastow a one-day warning before it would announce a credit-rating downgrade. Fastow's finance team went into crisis mode and by the end of the day Fastow had convinced Moody's that Enron's financial situation had been misrepresented.[113]

The moment Skilling anxiously awaited arrived at the end of January. Enron's stock price began to steadily climb upward: $41 on January 30, $42 on February 2, $43 on February 12, $44 on February 18, $45 on February 19, $46 on February 25, and $47 on February 27—a 15 percent increase in one month. On April 14, when Enron's stock price closed at $50, an ecstatic Lay gave each employee a $50 bill as a souvenir.[114] He promised to double their annual salary in Enron shares of stock if the company hit its performance targets for several years. Everyone's attention was now fixated on Enron's stock price momentum.

The substance behind the stock price increase was the expanding success of Lay and Skilling's business plan. Deregulation of California's electricity went into effect in 1998. Business was thriving, including a high-profile $60 million contract with Pacific Bell Park, home to the San Francisco Giants baseball team.[115] Success in California meant potential success in other parts of the country exploring deregulation models.

The stock market was finally catching up to Enron's entrepreneurial leadership. Fastow's creative financing enabled Skilling to survive the sunk cost investment phase, something Skilling failed to achieve as a high school and college student pursuing a risky stock market investment strategy. In March, when Skilling's first two choices for the vacated chief financial officer (CFO) position were either unavailable or performed poorly during the interview process, Skilling offered the CFO position to Fastow, who had actively lobbied for the job and even threatened to quit.[116] Some managers questioned Skilling's choice because Fastow was known for dealmaking rather than managerial skills, but they respected Skilling's desire to form an upper-management team composed of loyalists.

When professional gamblers finally hit a winning streak, they face a major dilemma: should they pay off old debts or continue to push their luck while there is luck to be had. Skilling chose the latter strategy. He thrived on the excitement of risk-taking and offered assistance to employees searching for new markets to conquer, including his former competitor for COO, Rebecca Mark.

In May, Skilling removed Mark as CEO of the International Division and terminated the deal-size bonus system that made her wealthy.[117] Mark explored other opportunities and decided to pioneer Enron's entry into the water industry. She convinced Enron to pay $2.4 billion for the very profitable Wessex Water, located in southwestern England. Enron renamed the company "Azurix" and made Mark its CEO in July.[118] Enron was now in the $300 billion water industry with its dealmakers exploring innovative ways to trade water. Capturing 20 percent of the market, a universal goal within Enron, would translate to an additional $60 billion in revenue.[119] This put Mark in a do-or-die situation, with Skilling monitoring her every move.

Funding the World's Transformation with SPEs: 1998

The overall strategic pieces seemed to be fitting in place. Enron now had operations related to three basic human survival resources—heat, electricity, and water. Lay successfully situated Enron as a key player in the world's transformation. Doors to world leaders opened even further for Lay to explore new ways to develop more efficient and effective distribution methods. Lay, Skilling, and Mark were at center stage in providing for the basic needs of people across the globe and establishing the infrastructure for the continued success of their version of global capitalism.

Skilling set his sights on Brazil as the cornerstone for

Enron's South American strategy. Enron bid on the government's sixth-largest electric power plant and purchased it for $1.3 billion. But Mark looked foolish when the bids were publicly announced because Enron's bid was nearly double the next highest offer. Enron could have owned the power plant for $600,000 less than it paid.[120]

More new market investments meant more financial manipulations to survive the substantial startup costs. Enron spent more than $3.5 billion on its two new international investments in the Brazilian electricity and British water markets. Wall Street lacked patience and punished firms that fell short of ever-increasing revenue and earnings projections. Enron needed some positive numbers right away.

To achieve 1998 sales of $31 billion, Skilling and Fastow relied on what worked for them in the past. Skilling inflated revenue by applying mark-to-market accounting techniques to the new trading ventures, even though the 1992 SEC ruling limited its use to the Gas Bank.[121] In addition, Enron accountants more favorably reevaluated company assets. For instance, Enron owned 40 percent of Promigas, a publicly traded Colombian gas pipeline firm. When Promigas's stock increased, Enron reclassified the business from a long-term strategic property to a merchant investment, which allowed Enron to change the firm's accounting method and claim even higher economic value.[122] Wall Street analysts who questioned Enron's actions paid a steep price. Even Merrill Lynch fired a research analyst for assessing Enron too harshly.[123]

Something had to be done right away to improve the appearance of Mark's spending spree. Fastow created an SPE named "Marlin," funded mostly with Enron stock, to purchase some of Enron's Wessex investment. Marlin removed $800 million of debt from Enron's balance sheet. Institutional investors then paid Marlin $1 billion for the debt and other assets guaranteed by Enron stock.[124] The Marlin SPE came with an important payment trigger. Those owning Marlin's debt could demand immediate repayment if Enron's stock price dropped below $37.84 and Enron's credit rating reached junk bond status, a scenario Skilling and Fastow considered very unlikely.[125]

Fastow was challenged to improve the appearance of domestic investments as well. In October, Fastow raised $1.5 billion in equity and debt so Enron could purchase three power plants in New Jersey. He then created an SPE to purchase a 50 percent stake in the plants, which enabled him to put the debt on the SPE's, rather than Enron's, balance sheet.[126]

Stock Price Success: 1998 and 1999

By now Fastow had created more than one thousand SPEs doing business with, or on behalf of, Enron. The SPEs, funded primarily with Enron stock, would remain healthy as long as Enron's stock remained healthy. But if Enron's stock declined significantly and margin calls needed to be met, the SPEs would have great difficulty making their loan payments and they would be forced to pay off the multitude of people whose SPE investments were guaranteed by Fastow. Enron would then have to put the SPE's debts on its balance sheets, which would further drive down the value of Enron's stock. In other words, everything could implode in an instant. However, Fastow and others believed that it was just a matter of time before Enron earned huge profits from its many endeavors, and that money could be used to clean up the SPE mess.

Fastow's illegal SPEs continued to pad Enron's annual net income. In 1998, they added $133 million to revenue and kept $561 million of debt off Enron's balance sheets.[127] The recording of onetime nonrecurring asset sales as recurring income from operations accounted for 40 percent of Enron's annual earnings.[128] Negative second- and third-quarter cash flows were once again miraculously transformed into the positive column, and Enron ended the fourth quarter with a very impressive $1.6 billion cash flow balance.[129]

Fastow rewarded himself by creating a change in a contract between Enron and Chewco, which forced Enron to pay Chewco a $400,000 nuisance fee. Kopper, Chewco's CEO, transferred $67,224 of this amount to the tax-exempt Fastow Family Foundation, a Houston charitable organization created by Fastow that participated in several SPE deals. The payment was kept hidden from both Fastow's accountants and the IRS. The Fastow Family Foundation then reimbursed the Fastows for business meetings in exotic locales, where little time was spent on business and a lot of time on vacationing.[130]

Enron's stock closed the year at $57.10 a share, a whopping 48 percent increase from its January 8 low of $38.50. The financial numbers were so good that huge trading profits made during a summer heat wave in the Midwest were set aside to boost results for the first quarter of 1999.[131] Skilling and Fastow were poised to guide Enron's stock on its upward trajectory.

Lay and Skilling initiated a buying spree in January 1999 that would eventually result in forty-one mergers and acquisitions over the next two years. For Fastow, this meant a lot more debt to finance. For Wall Street investment bankers, this meant $237.7 million in fees from Enron for 1999 alone.[132] For investors, this meant Enron was indeed on track to become the world's leading energy company. By the end of January, Enron's stock ballooned nearly 16 percent, to $66 a share.

After reporting a negative $660 million cash flow for the first quarter of 1999, Fastow became even bolder in his creation of interlocking SPEs to support Enron's growth strategy, transforming the new debt into cash. He created an SPE called "Osprey," leveraged by several Enron power plant holdings, to purchase 50 percent of Whitewing, an Enron subsidiary. This removed Whitewing's debt from Enron's balance sheets.[133] Whitewing then purchased several of Enron's underperforming power plants with the intent to resell. This increased Enron's revenue and removed bad assets from Enron's balance sheets. But why would anyone want to purchase Enron's underperforming assets? Fastow guaranteed Whitewing investors that he would make up any financial losses they incurred with an equivalent amount of Enron's increasingly valuable stock.[134]

Riding the Bull Market: 1999

Skilling and Fastow were definitely on a roll as they continued to turn losing investments into balance sheet winners. In 1999 the stock price declined for Promigas, the Colombian gas pipeline Enron owned, and Enron opened a brokerage account in Colombia. Then Enron employees bought substantial amounts of Promigas stock near the end of every quarter. The increase in demand in the relatively small stock market resulted in a rise in Promigas's stock price, which looked good on Enron's balance sheets.[135]

The stock market was also on a roll. The Federal Reserve Board added fuel to an already hot stock market by cutting interest rates in late 1998 to prevent the worldwide economic downturn from creeping into the U.S. economy. At the end of March, the Dow Jones Industrial Average rose above 10,000 for the first time ever, having doubled in value since 1995. In addition, startup companies like TheGlobe.com, which lost $11.5 million on just $2.7 million of revenue, saw their IPO stock jump from $9 to $87 on the first day of trading.[136]

Enron wanted a bigger piece of the IPO action. In June, Enron raised $695 million in cash by spinning off Azurix, Enron's British water subsidiary managed by Mark, as an IPO. Merrill Lynch earned $25 million for investment banking fees related to the IPO offering. Mark's Azurix stock options were now worth $50 million.[137] Skilling claimed the money generated from the IPO for Enron, hurting Azurix's operating budget.[138] Enron had been supporting Mark long enough; she now had to prove her managerial abilities in a difficult situation.

Day traders were significantly impacting market prices,

and many investors purchased stocks to take advantage of the stock market's momentum rather than buying based on a company's actual financial performance. Shortly after Amazon.com reported $50 million in losses, its stock price jumped from a seemingly overvalued $100 a share to a pre-stock split value of $400 a share.[139] The market was in a state of euphoria, and Enron was very well situated to remain a beneficiary.

Skilling, wanting to claim even more of this stock momentum, invested $1 billion to jump-start Enron's broadband activities. With technology experts declaring a doubling of Internet traffic every 100 days, Skilling envisioned trading bandwidth—access on the underground cables that carry Internet data from one computer to another. Enron had expertise in trading natural gas, water, and electricity—why not add bandwidth, a commodity central to the new economy. The $1 billion broadband investment, accompanied by selling Enron's holdings in an exploration and production subsidiary for $600 million cash, sent a strong message to employees: Enron's future success would be grounded in trading commodities, not brick-and-mortar businesses.[140]

These activities contributed to Enron's soaring stock price, which reached $80 in mid-June, a 40 percent increase since January. An Enron executive with $1 million worth of stock in January had an additional $400,000 in income six months later to leverage as collateral for purchasing real estate, cars, and other interests.

Buying Help from the LJMs: April through June 1999

The second half of the 1990s saw an abundance of overvalued dot.com IPOs. With the bull market in full force at the dawn of the Internet revolution, entrepreneurs were creating technology companies with assistance from venture capital-

ists who provided not only money but also a network of contacts to prepare the firms for public offerings. Investors
wanted to obtain stock prior to the official IPO, watch the
stock skyrocket through a speculation bubble, and then cash
out before the stock price collapsed. Enron hit the jackpot
with Rhythms NetConnections, an Internet service provider.
Enron purchased 5.4 million pre-IPO shares at $1.85 for a $10
million equity investment.[141] Rhythms NetConnections went
public on April 7, 1999. The stock ended its first day of trading at $69 a share. Enron's initial $10 million investment was
now worth more than $372 million.

During May 1999, Rhythms NetConnections stock
decreased to about $56, reducing the value of Enron's invest-
ment to $300 million. In order to help Enron meet its second-
quarter goals, Skilling wanted to claim the $290 million profit
as a part of recurring income before the stock price went
lower.[142] But pre-IPO investors had a legal obligation to hold
the stock for six months after the public offering before selling it. One possible way around this problem would be for
Enron to buy a "put option" from someone who would guarantee purchasing the Rhythms NetConnections stock at the
current $56 price when the six-month holding period ended.
However, most investors assumed that the Rhythms NetConnections stock price would decline, so the cost of buying a put
option on the open market was very high.

Not to be deterred at a time when Enron's stock price
continued its daily ascent, Fastow designed an intricate solution to Skilling's problem. He proposed creating an SPE
called "LJM1" (named after his wife Lea and sons Jeff and
Matthew), which could sell Enron a put option at a more reasonable price. The put option would obligate LJM1 to purchase the Rhythms NetConnections stock on demand for $56
a share between November 1999 and June 2004. If the stock
price went higher than $56 (plus the cost of the put option),
Enron could sell Rhythms NetConnections on the open market at the higher price and claim the additional profit. If the

stock price went below $56, Enron could exercise the put
option and force LJM1 to purchase the stock at $56. In both
scenarios, Enron came out a winner thanks to Fastow.

The creation of LJM1 could also help Enron maintain its
stock price momentum by purchasing Enron's underperforming assets whenever Enron needed a revenue boost to meet
quarterly targets. But enticing investors to participate in LJM1
would be a hard sell. Investors are not typically attracted to
companies that purchase financially troubled power plants and
sell very risky hedges. The key was making LJM1 appealing
enough to attract the 3 percent outsider equity necessary for
SPE status. This could be achieved by creating the usual complicated multilayers of SPEs financially supporting each other.

Fastow recommended funding LJM1 with 3.4 million
shares of Enron stock worth $276 million (about $81 a share)
and cash from three outside investors: $7.5 million from
Credit Suisse First Boston (CSFB), $7.5 million from
National Westminster Bank (NatWest), and $1 million from
LJM Partners. NatWest and CSFB, both of which had previous profitable dealings with Fastow, could serve as limited
partners and LJM Partners as a general partner. Then LJM1
could create an SPE called "LJM Swap Sub" by using 1.6 million of the 3.4 million shares of stock LJM1 received from
Enron and $3.75 million of the $16 million LJM1 received
from its outside investors. The SPE LJM Swap Sub could then
sell Enron the put option. The obligation to pay Enron $56 a
share for the Rhythms NetConnections stock would then
belong to LJM Swap Sub rather than LJM1, making LJM1 a
much more attractive investment to other outsiders.[143]

For this solution to work, Fastow would have to be
actively engaged in managing the LJM1 network of SPEs. He
offered to invest $1 million in LJM1 (which would thus
become LJM Partners) and to serve as director of LJM Swap
Sub, in return for a $500,000 annual salary from LJM1 and
half the profits on other assets owned by LJM1.[144] Given the
3.4 million shares of Enron stock in the LJM1 system, LJM1's

economic well-being was directly linked to Enron's economic well-being. Any price increase in Enron's stock above $81 would generate tremendous profit for LJM1 because it owned 3.4 million shares. Similarly, a decline in Enron's stock price would damage LJM1's economic performance.

The challenge for LJM1 was determining a put option price low enough to be affordable for Enron to hedge its bet on the Rhythms NetConnections stock, yet high enough to minimize the loses LJM1 would incur if the Rhythms Net-Connections stock dramatically declined. The price determination tension highlighted Fastow's conflict of interest. As Enron's CFO, he had a legal obligation to buy a hedge from LJM1 at the lowest price possible for a hedge. As LJM1's partner, he had a legal obligation to sell a hedge to Enron at the highest price possible. To offset anyone's concern that the relationship would favor LJM1 because of his involvement, Fastow proposed hiring the PricewaterhouseCoopers accounting firm to supply an opinion letter certifying its fairness.

Vince Kaminski, head of Enron's research group within RAC, was charged with analyzing the deal from Enron's perspective. As a favor to Fastow, Enron's chief accounting officer Rick Causey requested that Kaminski price the deal according to the wishes of Fastow, otherwise Enron would have to buy a hedge on the open market at an astronomical price. Kaminski opposed the arrangement and concluded that the deal heavily favored LJM1 at the expense of Enron.[145] If Enron's stock price should decline, which happens to all stocks now and then, LJM1 would not have the cash to pay $56 a share for the Rhythms NetConnections stock because LJM1 was funded primarily with Enron stock, which would now be worth a lot less. That meant Enron could claim a huge profit in the present moment, but then lose its entire investment and never receive any cash from LJM1 if Enron's stock price dropped too low. It would cause a balance sheet disaster.

Skilling ignored Kaminski's advice. For eight years Fastow helped to bail out Skilling quarter after quarter by creating more than a thousand SPEs that were clearly aligned with Enron's interests. Fastow had earned his mentor's unwavering trust. In addition, Skilling optimistically assumed that Enron's stock price would continue to multiply upward, providing LJM Swap Sub with more than enough money to purchase the Rhythms NetConnections stock. As a result, Skilling obtained Lay's approval to waive Enron's Code of Ethics so that Fastow, the company's chief financial officer, could invest in LJM1— a company that did business with Enron.

The final step in the approval process required sign off by Enron's board of directors. At the June 28, 1999 board meeting—attended by Lay, Skilling, Enron's chief risk officer Rick Buy, and David Duncan of Arthur Andersen—Fastow explained how Enron needed to hedge its Rhythms NetConnections stock, and the only available seller of a put option was LJM1. Furthermore, outside investors would only invest in LJM1 if Fastow invested in the SPE and served as its managing partner. To address concerns about the potential conflict of interest, all deals between Enron and LJM1 would be presented to the board for final approval. As a final safeguard, unlike many other SPEs, LJM1's financial statements would be audited by a public accounting firm—KPMG, not Arthur Andersen.

> *DECISION CHOICE.* If you were an Enron
> board member would you:
>
> (1) allow Enron to claim the Rhythms NetConnec
> tions profits by exempting Fastow from Enron's
> Code of Ethics, given the established accounting
> safeguards; or
>
> (2) allow Enron to lose its Rhythms NetConnec
> tions profits by refusing to exempt Fastow and, as
> a result, letting the entire LJM1 plan collapse?
>
> Why?

Andy Fastow as CFO of the Year: July through September 1999

The board supported the proposed arrangements and exempted Fastow from Enron's Code of Ethics.[146] In so doing, the board overlooked one important detail: by law SPEs required an independent manager, whereas LJM1 was being managed by Enron's CFO. Since LJM1 was not a legitimate SPE, it should have been accounted for as an Enron subsidiary. The LJM1 SPE was in clear violation of GAAP, and all of its debt should have been included on Enron's financial statements. Some Andersen auditors, including Carl Bass, went so far as to notify headquarter officials, but they were overruled by David Duncan.[147]

Although Enron executives and auditors seemed unconcerned about the potential conflict of interest, LJM1's outside investors were concerned. Which group of shareholders or partners would Fastow really be representing, Enron or LJM1?

One of the two primary outside investors, CSFB, concluded that Fastow would favor the interests of LJM1 because of the millions he would be earning in management fees as LJM1's general partner. Combined with his percentage of LJM1's profits, Fastow's LJM1 earnings would far exceed his Enron salary. Assuming a $300 million fund and the typical 2 percent management fee, Fastow stood to earn at least $6 million annually from LJM1.[148]

Representatives of CSFB warned Fastow that this financial arrangement would appear to be inappropriate if exposed to the media's glare, but they invested nonetheless. They did not want to cross Fastow, plus they also were positioned to make millions of dollars from the arrangement.[149] Fastow registered the new LJM1 partnership in the Caymans, which would make it exempt from U.S. taxes.[150] All his adult life, Fastow had rubbed elbows with wealthy fund managers. Now he would be one of them.

As for Kaminski, the lone internal voice of objection, Skilling transferred his entire research group so they could not obstruct future transactions. Skilling complained that Kaminski's group took its watchdog functions too seriously.[151] After six weeks of operation Fastow paid himself $550,000 in management fees from LJM1, covering half his initial $1 million investment in the fund. He anticipated much more money coming his way in the near future.[152]

Fastow's creative financing efforts were widely acclaimed, earning him *CFO Magazine's* 1999 CFO Excellence Award. The award-nominating idea originated from Fastow himself, who pushed Enron's public relations office to lobby the magazine editors on his behalf.[153] Fastow's praiseworthy accomplishments included funding the previously faltering Dabhol facility. In order to fund Phase Two of the project, Fastow's team put together five different loans totaling $1.4 billion and $452 million equity investment from banks in India, the United States, and Japan. Enron's investment in Dabhol now totaled $2.9 billion.[154] Mark and a few other top managers shared bonuses based on 3 to 4 percent of the net present value of the deal, which meant splitting about $30 million.[155]

With the third quarter coming to a close, Fastow used his management of LJM1 to pull off a major coup that enabled Enron to meet quarterly targets. Enron owned a power plant being built in Ciuaba, Brazil that was suffering from cost overruns and environmental problems associated with development of the tropical rain forest. The search for an independent third party to take on some of the financial burden had proven fruitless. On September 30, 1999, the last day of the third quarter, Fastow arranged to have LJM1 purchase a 13 percent interest in the facility for $11.3 million.

The sale allowed Enron to transfer Ciuaba's liabilities to LJM1's balance sheets and to change the accounting methods applied to the twenty-year gas supply contract, which resulted in an additional $34 million in mark-to-market income.[156] Fastow, protecting his own financial interests in LJM1, agreed to the deal only after Causey verbally agreed to buy back LJM1's investment at a profit upon demand.[157] If Arthur Andersen detected the scam, Ciuaba's liabilities would have to be put back on Enron's balance sheets because Enron remained fully at financial risk for Ciuaba's liabilities. The likelihood of this happening seemed slim because Arthur Andersen focused more on ensuring that appropriate fraud detection systems were in place than on actually detecting fraud.

More Complaints about Fastow: October 1999

Kaminski was not the only person questioning the appropriateness of Enron's CFO being a general partner in a firm doing business with Enron. He was joined by Enron executives who were part of Skilling's inner circle, including Ken Rice and Cliff Baxter, CEO of Enron North America.[158] The conflict of interest was so blatant that LJM's mailing address was Enron's headquarters and LJM employees shared offices with Enron negotiators; both were answerable to Fastow, who was responsible for their performance evaluations. Fastow encouraged Enron to sell assets to LJM without obtaining competitive bids from real third parties. When Enron did obtain competitive bids, Fastow demanded to know how much the competition bid so he could underbid them.[159]

Skilling refused to listen to their concerns. He trusted that Fastow had Enron's best interests in mind and gave Fastow permission to recruit investors for a second investment fund, LJM2. The professional staff of LJM2 included Fastow's protégés Michael Kopper and Ben Glisan, both of whom were on the Enron payroll. Fastow's selling points were LJM1's success record, his exemption to Enron's Code of Ethics, being privy to special deals, and an anticipated 30 percent return on investment.[160] Fastow had Enron's blessing to raise

$200 million through LJM2.[161]

Fastow once again targeted Tier 1 banks.[162] If these banks wanted to maintain or receive Tier 1 status, they were advised, they needed to invest in LJM2, otherwise they would be dropped down to Tier 3 when Enron went looking for an investment bank to arrange the next bond deal or acquisition. First Union invested $25 million, Canadian Imperial Bank of Commerce (CIBC) $15 million, J. P. Morgan $15 million, Chase Manhattan $10 million, CSFB $10 million, Citigroup $10 million, Lehman Brothers $10 million, Donaldson, Lufkin & Jenrette $5 million, and Merrill Lynch $5 million. Merrill Lynch employees individually kicked in an additional $17.6 million.[163]

Several bankers complained to Enron that Fastow had pressured them to invest, while others considered it an excellent investment opportunity. Those who raised their concerns directly with Skilling concluded that Enron's COO seemed well informed about Fastow's LJM2 activities.[164] Altogether, Fastow raised $392 million from fifty-one investors, double his initial goal, including $3.9 million of his own money.

There was one other major benefit for LJM2. When Enron's board approved LJM2 on October 11, 1999, Fastow worked it out so he could make deals between LJM2 and Enron without being slowed down by board approval. Instead, oversight would be provided by Skilling, Causey, and Buy.[165] All three Enron executives were already linked to Fastow activities. Causey had already agreed to one of Fastow's verbal LJM side-deals and Buy had quieted subordinates who objected to the LJM arrangements.[166] Fastow lied to the board when asked the amount of time he spent working for the LJMs—he claimed only three hours a week—and used his Enron staff to perform LJM transactions.[167]

All of this was unknown to the Arthur Andersen auditing engagement team. Nonetheless, Carl Bass continually questioned Enron's accounting methods. He decided to remove himself from direct involvement with the Enron account, and joined Arthur Andersen's PSG, which would give him even greater authority to provide guidance on contentious issues. Given his years of experience with Enron's accounting methodologies, Bass became the natural choice to offer a ruling on SPE deals, advice Duncan typically ignored.[168]

Lay and Skilling expected Enron's stock price to continue to multiply. They split the stock in 1999 in order to maintain a level of affordability. All previous stockholders doubled their total shares, though each share was worth half of its previous value. Shortly after the stock split, the stock price escalation stalled. Stock that had increased in value by 40 percent the first half of the year stabilized at about $40 during the second half of the year. Once again, Enron's negative cash flow status after three quarters needed to be inverted.

Nigerian Barges for Sale: October through December 1999

Mark's international business dealings, particularly the evaporation of water industry profits, contributed to Enron's stock problem. Azurix, burdened by high overhead costs, was outmaneuvered on several important competitive bids by two French companies. When Argentina privatized its water system, Mark outbid her competitors for the water company. Unfortunately for Enron, she bid $438.6 million for the water company when the next highest bid was only $150 million, costing Enron an extra $288 million for the purchase. Altogether, Mark overbid her competitors by more than $1 billion during this buying spree.

Making matters worse, Mark's purchase in Argentina did not include the water company's main office building, and the company's recordkeeping was in shambles. A national crisis arose when Argentineans, many of whom opposed the concept of privatizing water, began complaining about the taste of Azurix-supplied water. Azurix's stock dropped 40 percent when investors were informed that fourth-quarter profit targets would be missed.[169] The Argentina fiasco reaffirmed Skilling's belief that Enron's future should be trading commodities, not owning companies.

Skilling's disappointment with Enron's stock price was slightly offset when the company's first foray in the Internet was successful. On November 29, 1999, Enron Online went online. Energy trades could be made online rather than over the telephone. In addition to buying and selling energy, Enron now served as the middleman, taking a little piece of every energy trade.[170] The initial startup costs were huge, involving more than 350 employees, but so was the payout. Enron catapulted itself into the hottest investment arena—Internet companies—and the new business gave Enron an insider's view of competitor trading practices. Once again, Enron was one step ahead of everyone else. Within just a few months Enron Online would become the biggest e-commerce site on the Internet.[171]

With the year coming to a close, Fastow orchestrated seven deals in eleven days between Enron and the LJMs to provide Enron with some badly needed cash. These deals, which increased Enron's revenue by $229.5 million, enabled different business units to meet quarterly projection targets.[172] Fastow was now everyone's savior.

The accounting methods used for many of these deals violated GAAP, but Fastow and Causey had previously violated GAAP without being caught. For instance, Enron booked $16 million in profit when LJM2 paid $30 million for 75 percent of a malfunctioning power plant Enron owned in Poland. Why would LJM2 agree to such a deal? They had nothing to lose because Enron verbally agreed to repurchase the malfunctioning power plant for $32 million the following quarter, generating a $2 million profit for LJM2.[173] In the heat of negotiations, Fastow demanded that an Enron lawyer be dismissed for bargaining too hard on Enron's behalf.[174]

So many quick deals had to be made to support Enron's stock price that Fastow needed participation from companies not under his direct control. He first targeted Merrill Lynch, the nation's largest brokerage firm. Merrill Lynch earned $40 million in investment banking fees from Enron in the previous two years. Fastow requested that Merrill Lynch create a company called "Ebarge" to purchase three electricity-generating power barges off the coast of Nigeria that no one else wanted. A $28 million sale price would generate $12 million in profits for Enron, improve Enron's cash flow from operations, and enable the business unit to meet its projected targets.

> *DECISION CHOICE. If you were a Merrill Lynch investment banker earning large fees from doing business with Enron and were contacted by Andy Fastow to participate in Ebarge with guaranteed profits would you:*
>
> *(1) accept the offer,*
>
> *(2) reject the offer and risk losing future fees from Enron, and/or*
>
> *(3) notify Arthur Andersen about these secret side agreements?*
>
> *Why?*

A $40 Billion Banner Year: December 1999

The Merrill Lynch negotiating team was listening, but it thought the $28 million purchase price was too high. Fastow, needing to generate $12 million in profits, proposed supplying Merrill Lynch with $21 million toward the purchase price; Merrill Lynch would only have to come up with $7 million. In addition, Enron would pay Merrill Lynch $250,000 in cash for taking on this transaction and promised to buy back the barges in six months at $7,525,000 if a legitimate buyer could not be located, a nice profit of 22 percent per annum. And, of course, Merrill Lynch's participation would assure that it would be given prime investment banking deals in the future. The final agreement, a clear violation of what GAAP referred to as the parking of assets, was reached with two days left in the year.[175]

As always, the guaranteed buyback was not included in the written agreement. An Enron employee was severely reprimanded for including aspects of the oral agreements in notes from the meeting. Having achieved their financial goals, Enron executives were now qualified to receive their annual bonuses.[176]

Fastow's year-end wheeling and dealing helped Enron achieve $40 billion in revenue, a very impressive 28 percent increase from the previous year.[177] Earnings were up 18 percent.[178] The SPEs solved Enron's cash flow problem, providing more than $300 million in cash on the very last day of the year.[179]

The Dow Jones Industrial Average ended the year at an all-time high and Enron's stock price increased nearly 50 percent during the year. Fastow's LJMs and Chewco inflated Enron's profits by $248 million, one-fourth of its entire yearly profits, and hid $685 million of debt. One-third of Enron's pretax profits were attributed to projected earnings from mark-to-market accounting techniques.

Enron's 200 highest-paid executives earned $402 million, more than doubling the amount they earned the previous year. Lay's 1999 salary was $1.3 million with bonuses of $5.1 million. He owned 5.4 million shares of Enron stock worth $380 million. Skilling received an $850,000 salary and bonuses of $3 million. He owned 2.3 million shares of stock worth approximately $160 million.[180] In addition, Skilling renegotiated his contract with Lay, extending it to 2003. A clause in Skilling's new contract stipulated full payment of the four-year contract if he was not promoted to CEO of Enron by the end of 2000.

Many people owed a big thanks to Andy Fastow, whose reported family annual income reached $9.1 million—up from $2.2 million the previous year.[181] After only five months of operation, Fastow earned $5.3 million in management fees from LJM1, and his $1 million investment was worth $17 million.[182] Unlike some of his brothers-in-law, Fastow earned his millions through his own creativity. So 1999 was indeed a banner year, and he expected 2000 to be even better.

Broadband Rollout: January 2000

Enron's stock price increased 14 percent during the first week of 2000, a great start to a year filled with high hopes. Everyone geared up for Enron's January 20 analyst conference, an event that would resemble a Broadway show opening. At the annual conference, upper-level managers wined and dined people who advised investors on what stocks to buy. The focus of this year's event would be Enron's full immersion into the broadband industry. The Internet would become better and faster for all users because of Enron Broadband Services (EBS).

The year 2000 would be the dawn of a new millennium shaped by the Internet and computers. Skilling positioned Enron to jump to the front of the Internet gold rush, prepared to battle head-to-head against AT&T, WorldCom, and other telecommunication giants. The new millennium also had new rules that Enron had been operating under for over a decade:

Internet investors cared about revenue, not profits. Don't worry about profits, increase revenue no matter the cost, scare away the competition, and then start cutting costs. Jeff Bezos, the CEO of Amazon.com, earned "Man of the Year" honors from *Time* magazine in December, despite experiencing a 437 percent increase in losses.[183]

Well-financed e-businesses were popping up everywhere and traditional companies wanted to reinvent themselves on the Internet. Skilling's one-day challenge was to convince research analysts and stock portfolio managers that EBS could capture 20 percent of the broadband market as the stock market entered its unprecedented ninth year of economic expansion.[184]

Enron choreographed a dynamic script for the January 20 rollout. Ken Rice, who initially impressed Skilling by piecing together the $1.3 billion New York Power Authority contract back in 1990, had agreed to serve as co-CEO of the broadband division. He would announce that EBS had an estimated worth of $29 billion and revenue projections of $54 million for 2000 and $280 million for 2001.[185] To establish immediate credibility with skeptical portfolio managers, Scott McNealy, the well-known CEO of Sun Microsystems, would unexpectedly appear to announce Enron's $350 million purchase of 18,000 top-of-the-line servers. Enron meant business right away so invest before the stock price skyrocketed![186]

Enron executives explored ways Enron could financially benefit from the anticipated stock price increase caused by these public announcements. The Fastow-created SPE funded primarily with Enron stock, JEDI, had hedged its stock holdings. The benefit of hedging is that a third party makes up the financial difference if the stock price drops too low. On the other hand, the third party keeps the difference if the stock rises above an agreed-upon amount. Enron could reap a huge profit if the third party temporarily removed the upper price limit on January 20 and created a new upper limit the day after Enron's stock spiked. Naturally, no third-party hedger would agree to do this because it would be forfeiting its own profits. However, in this case, the third party was another Fastow-created SPE, so anything was possible. Fastow, Skilling, and Causey worked out the details and "Operation Grayhawk" was approved.[187]

On January 20, Enron's stock opened at $53.50. McNealy's surprise appearance delighted the crowd. Then Skilling, true to form, exaggerated a bit when he claimed that EBS already built its Internet network and all Enron had to do was turn on the switch.[188] He projected EBS would lose $100 million during its first year of operations, which seemed reasonable given the substantial startup costs. The flattered research analysts and stock portfolio managers responded on cue to the good news, driving Enron's stock price up to $67.30, an all-time high given the August 1999 two-for-one stock split, and a 26 percent increase in one day. Operation Grayhawk raked in $85 million of earnings.[189]

Fully aware that Skilling provided misleading information to the audience, Causey sold 45,000 shares for $3.2 million the following day when the stock price continued to climb, of which $800,000 was the result of the Rice/McNealy/Skilling performance at the January 20[h] conference.[190] Rice was also sitting pretty. Upon becoming CEO of EBS, Rice received a $1.75 million cash bonus and more than 1.7 million in stock options, 20 percent of which could be vested immediately.[191]

It was now full steam ahead for Skilling, Causey, Fastow, and their crew of well-paid loyalists. Enron was getting richer, and so were they, a perfect win-win situation.

The Southampton Place Arrangement: February and March 2000

Not everyone was on board. Any executive who took the time to study the details was shocked. Jeff McMahon, Enron's treasurer, joined the growing number of people complaining to both Skilling and Fastow about Fastow's LJM1 and LJM2 conflicts of interest.[192] Fastow and Michael Kopper wanted Enron's best assets at the lowest prices. Kopper represented the LJMs and, as a member of Enron's finance group, he knew Enron's lowest selling price on an asset before negotiations even began, and that was the price he demanded. McMahon received several complaints from Enron employees unwilling to negotiate too hard on deals with Fastow's SPEs because Fastow was responsible for their performance evaluation and compensation.[193]

McMahon had witnessed Fastow, his boss, lying about the SPEs on several occasions and sympathized with the Enron employees who either quit or requested transfers. He appealed to Skilling for help, but Skilling refused to become more actively involved in monitoring the transactions. Skilling framed the problem as a personality conflict between McMahon and Fastow, and sided with Fastow, the successful loyalist who had been bailing him out for almost a decade. Causey typically sided with Fastow and Kopper also. Skilling pressured McMahon to agree to the conditions they requested, maintaining that the transactions between Enron and the LJMs were legitimate, even though better deals could be obtained from legitimate third parties.

When Fastow learned that McMahon, his subordinate, had complained to Skilling, Fastow's boss, he confronted McMahon in a fit of rage.[194] Unwilling to deal with the extra anxieties, McMahon accepted reassignment to a different Enron division. This provided Fastow the opportunity to appoint another loyalist to the treasurer position. He chose Ben Glisan, who had previously worked on the LJM accounts, to deal with the banks on his behalf.[195] Whereas McMahon would not allow Kopper to profit more than $1 million from one particularly contentious transaction with Enron, Glisan approved a $10 million profit to Kopper for the same transaction. McMahon's reassignment earned Kopper and Fastow a quick $9 million.[196]

The money kept pouring in for Fastow and his co-conspirators. Fastow arranged for Enron to purchase RADR, an SPE he had relied on over the previous three years to help business units meet their projected revenue targets through end-of-quarter sales. Kopper earned $2.2 million from his RADR investment and sent a total of $125,000 in gift checks to the Fastow family.[197]

After reviewing some of Fastow's SPE arrangements, Skilling decided that Enron should sell its Rhythms NetConnections stock and liquidate the put option it had purchased from LJM Swap Sub.[198] Meanwhile, NatWest bankers were meeting with Fastow about selling the bank's interest in both LJM1 and LJM Swap Sub. NatWest was very pleased with its financial returns on the LJM1 investment. The bank assumed that its LJM Swap Sub investment had become worthless following the liquidation process. But the three bankers representing NatWest realized that the value of the Enron stock in the SPE had risen, creating additional revenue to be distributed. The three bankers shared some of Fastow's flawed character traits and proposed several ways to claim this money for themselves without NatWest's knowledge. Fastow was more than happy to accommodate them.

On March 20, Fastow created a new SPE called "Southampton Place," named after the exclusive neighborhood where he and other Enron executives lived. Its 3 percent outside investor equity consisted of a $750,000 loan from Chewco and relatively small investments from Kopper, the Fastow Family Foundation, Glisan (Enron's new treasurer), Enron attorney Kristina Mordaunt, and three other favored Enron/LJM employees who assisted him on these transactions.[199] Southampton Place purchased LJM Swap Sub and Fastow distributed the funds to its investors, including cooperative Enron employees willing to invest in an entity doing business with Enron.

In a very complicated set of accounting maneuvers,

Causey made a $30 million payment from Enron to buy out the LJM Swap Sub investors. Fastow allocated $20 million to NatWest and $10 million to CSFB, LJM Swap Sub's other major investor. The $20 million NatWest payment was distributed to NatWest ($1 million), the three NatWest bankers (total of $7.3 million), and Southampton Place ($11.7 million). Less than two months after the SPE had been created, the Southampton Place funds were distributed among Kopper and his domestic partner ($4.5 million for a $25,000 investment), the Fastow Family Foundation ($4.5 million for a $25,000 investment), Glisan ($1 million for a $5,800 investment), Mordaunt ($1 million for a $5,800 investment), and three other Enron/LJM employees (about $500,000 each).[200]

Financially, Fastow took very good care of Enron's new treasurer, making Glisan an instant millionaire. Whereas McMahon had previously complained about Fastow's schemes involving Enron employees, Glisan pocketed the cash. The future seemed very bright for Fastow's network of friends.

Then the dot.com bubble burst in April 2000 and the Internet bull market soon came to a screeching halt.

The Raptors: April through July 2000

Enron hit several pre-IPO investment jackpots in early 2000. Skilling wanted to immediately claim their current stock value, even though Enron could not legally sell them for several months. This sounded a lot like the initial Rhythms NetConnections situation and Fastow knew exactly what to do: create an SPE to hedge the investment. But who would create an obligation now to pay Enron $80 a share in 2005 for an Internet company's stock that, in all likelihood, could be bankrupt in the near future? Fastow's LJM2, of course, assuming favorable terms could be negotiated.

On April 18, Fastow created Raptor I, to hedge Enron's latest IPO stock.[201] Raptor I was funded with $527 million worth of Enron stock, and LJM2 served as the independent outside investor with $30 million in cash. Negotiations between Enron and LJM2 consisted of Glisan (awaiting a $1 million payout for his $5,800 investment in Southampton Place), representing Enron, and Kopper (awaiting a $4.5 million payout for his $25,000 investment in Southampton Place), representing LJM2. With the approval of both Skilling and Causey, Fastow arranged for Enron not only to reimburse LJM2's $30 million investment but also to guarantee an additional $11 million profit on the deal within six months. Enron wouldn't exercise the hedge if Fastow had anything to say about it, so Raptor I would never have to buy the IPO stock from Enron. Also, LJM2 would receive a $250,000 management fee from Enron. Furthermore, Enron agreed to pay all the accounting and legal fees associated with the deal.

Enron could immediately book IPO profits before its stock prices began their inevitable decline, and LJM2 investors would earn $11 million profit from selling the put option, a win-win situation for both parties. Arthur Andersen, ignorant of the side agreement, signed off on the deal. Given Andersen's approval, the board of directors had no objections. While LJM2 was initially expected to raise $200 million of outside capital, it attracted nearly $400 million in investments.[202]

The SEC's chairman, Arthur Levitt, believed that the large consulting fees that auditing firms received from clients compromised accounting standards through favorable accounting treatment. While auditing fees were capped and nonnegotiable in the competitive auditing marketplace, consulting fees were open-ended. Andersen earned $35 million in consulting fees from Enron, its largest client, compared to $14 million in auditing fees. Duncan charged $750 an hour for his services and oversaw the work of 140 auditors and consultants, each of whom charged billable hours to the Enron account. In return, Enron expected Duncan's cooperation on its aggressive accounting techniques.[203] The relationship between Andersen and Enron became so close that Lay submitted a letter to Levitt and the SEC criticizing a federal proposal to prohibit auditors from doing consulting work with the same client. Ironically, Lay had simply signed off on the letter, which had been ghostwritten by Duncan, the Andersen auditor.[204]

Enron further enshrined itself among investors by replacing General Electric as the winner of *Fortune* magazine's best-managed company in America.[205] But winning public relations awards did not translate into cash, and Enron's financial problems wouldn't cease. The company already had a negative $457 million cash flow from the first quarter, at a time when Wall Street investors were beginning to disinvest their Internet portfolios. With less than half the year over, EBS surpassed its projected $100 million in annual losses and raised the projected loss expectation to $500 million.[206] In addition, Enron was spending $300 million constructing a new office tower to house the increasing number of employees, many of whom received large salaries and costly benefits.[207] And, with no legitimate buyers in sight, Enron would soon have to buy back those three Nigerian barges from Merrill Lynch's Ebarge for $8 million.

Fastow, Causey, and Skilling did what they could to help business units meet their second-quarter projections. Like every company in the broadband industry, EBS had an oversupply of unused Internet cables, referred to as dark fiber. Ken Rice, the new CEO of EBS, and Fastow propped up the division's numbers by selling $100 million of dark fiber to LJM2, with the understanding that Enron would buy them back if a legitimate third-party buyer could not be located. This generated $53 million in pretax profits.[208] Enron drastically cut broadband prices to gain greater market share, making enemies of telecommunication competitors that were struggling to survive the bursting of the dot.com bubble.

Repeating the Nigerian barge success, Enron sold $36.5 million worth of airplanes to an SPE controlled by Bankers

Trust, with the guarantee that Enron would find a legitimate buyer after the quarter ended.[209] Expert use of mark-to-market accounting contributed to Enron's revenue, which reached $30 billion for the first six months. But even that was not enough for Wall Street investors. In mid-July, Skilling and Causey approved several accounting adjustments that enabled Enron to declare 34 cents earnings-per-share, two cents above analyst predictions.[210] Revenue was at an all-time high and earnings-per-share exceeded expectations in the midst of an economic downturn—take that Wall Street!

Over the next few months, Fastow created three new Raptors to enhance Enron's revenue, each funded with $30 million cash from LJM2. Fastow terminated a Raptor called "Porcupine" after only one week, earning $9.5 million on the $30 million investment.[211] Another Raptor was created to hedge Enron's stock holdings in Avici. Enron's $15 million investment in Avici's pre-IPO stock ballooned to $162 million. A high-tech stock's inevitable decline is usually obvious only after the fact, so Fastow and Causey cheated by backdating some Raptor put options to just prior to the IPO stock's decline.[212] Enron Broadband Services received $35 million in profits from this hedge transaction. [213]

Despite all these sleights of hand, Fastow still had to borrow $3.4 billion to pay operational expenses.[214] If only Enron could achieve huge revenues and profits from one of its many investments.

The Stock Price Summit: July and August 2000

California's weather problems were manna from heaven for Enron. The demand for electricity skyrocketed when temperatures in California soared to over 100 degrees during the summer of 2000. But Skilling could not boast about these profits publicly without jeopardizing Enron's advantage. If its profits were known, California politicians would demand a price cap and the rewriting of regulatory policies.

The state bureaucrats who developed California's electricity market deregulation policies were no match for Enron's savvy traders. One policy required payment to energy suppliers for withdrawing electricity from overburdened transmission lines. Making a financial killing off this policy was easy. Enron flooded 2,900 megawatts of power over a 15-megawatt transmission line, and earned additional revenue when the excess electricity was withdrawn. But the state desperately needed the electricity Enron withdrew, a demand that resulted in an immediate 70 percent price increase. This game-playing cost California ratepayers an additional $7 million.[215]

During periods of low demand and prices, mysterious operational problems made Enron's electric power unavailable. The operational problems were solved and the electric power became available again when prices rose. Another revenue-generating game played by Enron at the expense of California taxpayers entailed buying electricity in California at low prices, sending it north to Enron's Portland General facility, and then sending it back into California at higher out-of-state prices.

The electric energy traders developed creative names for these manipulative strategies, including "Death Star," "Ricochet," "Get Shorty," "Perpetual Loop," and "Fat Boy."[216] Enron relied on creative accounting techniques to prevent disgruntled consumers and politicians from determining its profits. But Californians rebelled, burned their electricity bills in public demonstrations, and state politicians initiated an investigation.[217]

Skilling wanted to impress upon Wall Street investors that Enron earned its profits from a steady income stream, rather than from market speculations, when just the opposite was true. In one day, an Enron trader made $60 million when electricity prices spiked during a heat wave. Another day, Enron traders lost $600 million when a cold spell unexpectedly drove energy prices down. In less than a month, one Enron trader went from being up $200 million to being down $200 million.[218]

Skilling and Causey created "Schedule C," an account that did not appear on Enron's balance sheet, in which to deposit excessive trading profits. "Schedule C" totaled more than $1 billion in unreported earnings. The hidden money was used to offset losses and help other business units meet their quarterly targets.[219]

Enron's stock price, which had been fluctuating between the mid-$60s and low-$70s since the end of January, received a boost in mid-July following the announcement of a twenty-year partnership with Dallas-based Blockbuster, the nation's largest video rental chain. The vision—videos on demand through the Internet—would be a dream come true for millions of movie fans. Customers could comfortably sit on a couch with a bowl of popcorn, turn on the television, screen through thousands of movie titles, and pick one for immediate viewing pleasure. Blockbuster would supply the movies and Enron the broadband connection to the house. The technology would be test-marketed in several cities, with Enron receiving $1.20 for every rental.[220]

Enron was now the hottest stock on Wall Street, increasing in value from $71.80 on July 25 to $90.56 on August 23, as investors took their capital out of failed dot.coms and put their money elsewhere. Given the 1999 stock split, that meant Enron stock purchased for $40 when Skilling became COO in March 1997 was now worth $181 a share. Skilling, a hero in the financial press, was now poised to take on CEO duties. Lay told Skilling that he would step aside in early 2001 and let Skilling steer the course of Enron's future.

Two days later, Rebecca Mark, Skilling's nemesis, resigned as CEO of Azurix, Enron's financially troubled international water-industry holding company. While Enron's stock price had achieved an all-time high, Azurix's stock price rose to $23 shortly after its initial public offering, only to drop to less than $7 a share.

Mark mismanaged the overpriced assets she had acquired. Her failed efforts in India and Argentina cost Enron $2 billion, with projected losses of $11.6 million for the year. Enron owned $7 billion in international assets, and the division's profits were a paltry $100 million, less than what could have been earned from a savings account at a bank.[221] Mark left Enron with a golden parachute. She also divested her stock options, cashing in a total of $82.5 million.[222]

Some companies discourage senior executives from cashing out their stock options, fearful of how investors might interpret it. Earlier in the year, Causey sold $3.2 million in stock options and he had much more vested. Skilling also had a large reserve of vested stock options. Occasional sell-offs are expected, but simultaneous large sell-offs by top executives might suggest to Wall Street analysts that Enron's stock had reached a momentary peak and bad news was on the horizon.

> *DECISION CHOICE. If you were an Enron senior executive with an overabundance of vested stock options, would you:*
>
> *(1) sell your stock options at the current high price, or*
>
> *(2) hold on to your stock options to demonstrate faith in the future of the company?*
>
> *Why?*

More Problems and Financial Schemes: September through December 2000

Other executives followed Mark's lead. During the first week of September, Skilling sold 86,000 shares for $7.4 million. Three weeks later, Causey sold more than 80,000 shares for $7.1 million.[223]

While executives cashed out some of their stock options, Fastow struggled with the ramifications of unprofitable business units, whose anticipated profits had been booked under mark-to-market accounting techniques. Enron planned on claiming $53 million in fourth-quarter profits based on the value of the Blockbuster partnership, but the technology necessary to deliver affordable video on demand proved difficult to develop.[224] Less than 5 percent of all Internet users had the high-speed connections necessary for downloading video in a reasonable amount of time.[225] According to Enron analysts, an unrealistic 50 million subscribers (one-half of all American households) were needed to break even, and this assumed that 75 percent of them rented six movies a week and 25 percent rented ten to fourteen movies a week.[226] It wasn't going to happen.

In addition, neither Blockbuster nor Enron could fulfill their contractual expectations with potential customers.[227] Blockbuster struggled to get contracts with movie companies they previously bullied, while Enron struggled to get contracts with telecommunications companies upset over its broadband price-cutting strategies. The Blockbuster-Enron partnership was quickly falling apart. Yet Enron needed the mark-to-market profits from the endeavor to meet quarterly profit projections.

Fastow spun his magic, turning yet another seemingly inevitable revenue loss into a revenue gain. He convinced Canadian Imperial Bank of Commerce, a Tier 1 bank, to invest $115.2 million in an SPE that purchased the next ten years of profits from the Blockbuster-Enron partnership. The deal enabled Enron to declare a combined $110 million in profits for the last quarter of 2000 and first quarter of 2001.[228] Fastow floated the idea of creating LJM3 to raise $2 billion under his management control, should Enron need the help.[229]

Enron had also claimed $42 million in mark-to-market profits during the Dabhol power plant's first year of operations. But, during 2000, the Maharashtra State Electricity Board (MSEB) refused to honor previously signed agreements guaranteeing energy purchases from the facility, even though MSEB owned a 15 percent share. Electricity consumption was far below expectations. The guaranteed purchases pushed MSEB to the edge of bankruptcy. After a blackout affected 200 million people, Enron played hardball and demanded three times its normal rate to restart the facility. However, India was not California, and government officials refused to be manipulated.[230] Enron stood to lose its $2.9 billion investment, which included $20 million of bonuses already paid to Enron executives for closing the initial deal.[231]

Mark's former division created other headaches as well. Cost overruns in Brazil reached $300 million and counting.[232] To earn favor with the Clinton Administration, Enron agreed to build a $140 million oil-fired power plant in Palestine. The project appealed to Lay's religious sentiments and vision of Enron as the energy leader ushering in world peace at the dawn of the new millennium. Unfortunately, the plant was bogged down by Middle Eastern political problems. Azurix's problems also continued to mount. When its stock price fell below $3.50 a share, Enron purchased back the company for $325.9 million to regain total control of operations.[233]

Given the escalating costs associated with the growing number of failures, Skilling attempted to sell off Enron's international assets. Cliff Baxter served as the high-level salesman, looking for someone to buy everything for $7 billion. He struck gold with a group of Middle Eastern investors. They verbally agreed on a price that would include $4 billion in desperately needed cash.[234] All but one of the appropriate signatures were obtained—the sheik who had final authority. The deal fell through when the sheik was unable to sign due to a severe medical problem. Baxter had to begin searching for a new buyer and there were no prospects in sight.[235]

In response to the spread of deregulated energy policies across the nation, Enron created New Power in partnership with AOL Time Warner and IBM, to provide electricity and gas resources at prices lower than those available from public utilities. Enron owned 45 percent of New Power and Lou Pai, a longtime Skilling loyalist, served as its Chairman. New Power's pre-IPO shares sold at $11, and they increased in value to $21 when New Power went public in October.

When the stock price reached $27 a share, Fastow hedged Enron's New Power stock with another Raptor. As usual, Fastow verbally agreed to cover any losses sustained by Raptor investors with Enron stock. Enron immediately claimed $16 a share in profits before the New Power's stock declined, which it did, to $10 a share by the end of the year.[236]

However, by early December Enron's stock price had dropped back down to $70 from its high of $90 three months earlier, and more stock would be required to support its hedges. With the year drawing to a close, senior executives searched for more revenue to meet earnings targets. Causey closed one business unit's financial shortfall by positively reevaluating an energy asset by an extra $100 million.[237]

Fastow and Skilling continued to be adventurous with prepay agreements that transformed loans into revenue. They worked out an agreement to sell $394 million of natural gas for a discounted $330 million over the next four years to Mahonia, a firm owned by J. P. Morgan Chase. Enron agreed to repurchase the natural gas from Mahonia in monthly installments costing a total of $394 million. This maneuver enabled Enron to claim an additional $330 million in revenue for 2000, while J. P. Morgan Chase earned a $64 million profit by temporarily parking the natural gas.[238]

Broadband activities provided other opportunities for wheeling and dealing. Enron's EBS division joined other broadband companies in an incestuous pursuit to mislead Wall Street investors by swapping dark fiber with each other to inflate revenue. "Dark fiber" refers to unused broadband cables, not yet lit up, which were laid underground or in the ocean in anticipation of continually expanding Internet usage. Telecommunication companies had overbuilt, and were looking for creative ways to claim revenue for these unused cables.

Enron claimed a $20.3 million finder's fee by helping LJM2—meaning Fastow—sell $40 million of dark fiber it had purchased from Enron a few months earlier.[239] Fastow also arranged a $113 million dark fiber sale between LJM2 and another SPE he created, earning LJM2 a $2.4 million profit.[240] The LJMs and Chewco enabled Enron to hide $628 million of debt for the year. EBS, in turn, sold $17 million in dark fiber to Global Crossing, which likewise sold $17 million in dark fiber to EBS, an even trade. Each firm immediately claimed the revenue and delayed reporting the expenditure.[241]

Fastow's greatest struggle was managing the Raptors that kept Enron's debt off its balance sheets. The complicated restructuring of all four Raptors not only invalidated the Raptors as legitimate SPEs, but also favored LJM1 at Enron's expense. After analyzing the arrangements, Vince Kaminski, the head of Enron's research group who had previously complained about Enron's relationship with LJM1 and Rhythms NetConnections, refused to sign off on the deal.[242] Nonetheless, Fastow had the full cooperation of David Duncan, head of Arthur Andersen's client engagement team, which earned $1.3 million providing accounting advice on the Raptor accounts.

Unknown to anyone involved, a major accounting error occurred during the restructuring process. Enron had issued $1 billion of stock to the Raptors for a promissory note, which enabled them to borrow against additional stock. Enron reported an increase in shareholder equity by the value of the stock it issued. However, such an increase can only be claimed if the stock is purchased with cash.[243]

Enron's aggressive accounting techniques were gaining the attention of other Arthur Andersen partners in the company's Chicago headquarters.[244] They rated the Enron engagement team a "two" on a five-point scale with "five" being the highest rating.[245] Carl Bass, still a PSG member, raised several objections regarding Fastow's use of SPEs. Bass specifically objected to the use of Raptor accounts to hedge IPO investments that were declining in value, such as Avici and New Power. The local auditing team ignored Bass's advice, enabling Enron to delay reporting $500 million in losses until the first quarter of 2001.[246]

End of the Year Acclaims: December 2000

The end result of all these activities was pleasing for Fastow, Skilling, Lay, and Enron—$100 billion in revenue, a 150 percent increase from the previous year, and $1.3 billion in reported profits. Causey hid more than $1 billion of California trading profits in a reserve that could be tapped in 2001.[247] Enron had signed contracts to manage the energy needs of more than 25,000 major customers worldwide. In addition, Enron paid no federal tax payments for the fourth time in five years, as the use of stock option accounting transformed a $112 million tax payment into a $278 million tax refund.[248] The board of directors was very pleased, and approved Skilling's promotion to succeed Lay as CEO.

With great acclaim, Enron climbed to #7 on the Fortune 500 list, between Citigroup and IBM.[249] Just four years after entering the market, Enron was the nation's largest supplier of electricity.[250] For the fifth consecutive year, Enron won *Fortune* magazine's most innovative company award. The company was ranked #22 among the "100 Best Companies to Work for in America," #25 for "Most Admired Company in the World," and #31 for "Fastest Growing Company."

And George W. Bush, Lay's political friend and donation beneficiary, would soon take over as president of the United States. Lay's fundraising skills for the Republican Party had earned him a seat among its inner circle. Enron donated $2.4 million to candidates running for national political office and an additional $300,000 for upcoming inauguration events.[251] The company expected some payback, in the form of more favorable federal deregulation policies and government subsidies.[252]

Enron executives continued to benefit from accounting manipulations. Lay received a $7 million bonus for Enron's rising profits and stock price during 2000, and a $3.6 million bonus for Enron's 294 percent increase in shareholder return on equity over the previous four years. Lay still owned $5.1 million in stock options that could generate $257.5 million in profits if he decided to cash them out.[253]

Other key players contributing to Enron's inflated stock price also benefited. Skilling sold more than $11 million in stock options during the first week of November. On November 15, he started selling 10,000 shares per week for the rest of the year, and would continue to do so for a total of thirty-two weeks.[254] Ken Rice, CEO of EBS, was in the process of selling 45,000 shares at a $2.6 million profit. Fastow's reported family income, $9.1 million the previous year, sky-rocketed to $48.6 million for 2000, with about 90 percent coming from the LJMs.[255]

Putting a damper on all this was one basic fact—if Enron's transactions had been appropriately accounted, the 2000 revenue would have been $6.3 billion, good for #287 on the Fortune 500 list, not $100 billion and a #7 ranking.[256] Only a few executives understood this. Forty percent of Enron's reported profits came from dealings with Fastow partnerships.[257]

Once again, similar to each of the previous ten years, the year 2001 could either make or break Enron. The firm had

20,000 employees with operations in more than forty nations. It had shot up the ranks of Fortune 500 firms and joined the corporate elite. Enron was poised to become #1 on the Fortune 500 list within the next few years, challenging the world's best organizations for global domination. Enron was reshaping national and international energy policies in a way that could generate cleaner energy at lower prices. But, from the perspective of Fastow, Causey, and Skilling—the major architects of Enron's meteoric rise—Enron's actual performance could ruin everything. They had skillfully managed public perceptions the past few years, but that couldn't last forever. Enron needed real revenue, real cash, and real profits.

Wall Street analysts would develop their 2001 revenue projections based on the $100 billion that Enron had publicly claimed for the previous year, rather than the $6.3 billion it had actually earned from its trades. The accounting was way out of control. Enron would have to somehow meet new analyst projections, derived from a faulty baseline, if it were to remain a hot stock.

CHAPTER 3

THE IMPLOSION YEAR

Skilling the CEO: January and February 2001

Skilling had helped save Enron in 1990 as CEO of Enron's Gas Bank. He, more than anyone else, was responsible for Enron's transformation from a regional natural gas pipeline company to the world's largest energy trading firm. In 1990, 80 percent of Enron's revenue came from the gas pipeline business. Now, with 95 percent of its revenue came from Enron's trading units, the company was called "The Goldman Sachs of Energy Trading."[258] A substantial and growing percentage of Enron's trading business consisted of very risky derivatives.[259]

Combined, Enron's four major service areas contained $3.9 trillion in untapped opportunities. It was now up to Skilling to funnel some of that money into Enron.[260] Both the broadband and energy trading markets had tremendous potential for future growth. Skilling predicted Enron's broadband market would reach $500 billion by 2005, so there was plenty of hope for future growth.[261] He told those attending the January analyst conference in Houston that Enron's stock was undervalued at $70, and predicted it would climb to $126 during his first year as CEO.[262] He estimated the stock value of the pipeline business unit at $6, the trading business unit at $23, the broadband business unit at $40, and the wholesale energy business unit at $57.[263] To the analysts' delight, Enron increased its profit estimates from $1.60 a share to $1.70.[264]

On February 12, 2001, Skilling, at age forty-eight, added CEO to his title as president of Enron, with the understanding that he could become chairman of the board at the end of the year, if all went well.[265] Internally, his performance would be benchmarked against Enron's stock price, which had risen to $80 a share. Ken Lay could now shed the burden of being a CEO and focus on being chairman of the board. His political connections deepened with the election of fellow Texan George W. Bush. Lay used Enron's corporate jet to fly former President George W. H. Bush and first lady Barbara Bush to their son's inauguration in the nation's capital.[266]

Lay's deregulation efforts led to White House meetings with the very receptive vice-president, Dick Cheney. Lay opposed federal intervention in the deregulated California electricity market. He garnered the support of leading Republicans to oppose political pressure from California to cap electricity prices after the state already had spent more than $8 billion buying electricity on the open market.[267] Trust the free market system, Lay and Skilling insisted.

Although Lay opposed federal intervention in the United States, he sought it in India. Lay followed the lead of many business leaders, favoring free market solutions when they are to their company's benefit, and opposing them otherwise. Enron was still providing energy in India, even though the Maharashtra State Electricity Board, the power plant's sole customer, had stopped paying for it the previous December. Enron's investment was too high for the company to just pull out, so Lay appealed for help from his White House friends. The federal government had a major stake in the issue because OPIC provided $391.8 million worth of insurance and the Export-Import Bank provided $302 million in loans for the Dabhol power facility.[268]

Lay had several political options. He had earned enough local support to be considered a serious contender for mayor of Houston, having donated his time and Enron's resources for the benefit of city residents. Enron donated 1 percent of pretax earnings to local charities, which amounted to $12 million in 2000, including $5 million to the city's United Way campaign. During the past few years, Enron had donated $13 million to the city's colleges and universities, $2 million to the performing arts, $1.4 million to high school scholarships, and $1 million to the YMCA, which named a center after Lay.[269] Lay also encouraged other employees to participate in philanthropic activities. Enron employees raised $500,000 in pledges for a Houston-to-Austin bike race benefiting the Multiple Sclerosis Society. Jeff Skilling led the pack with $65,000 in pledges.[270]

Yet much of Lay's financial net worth was tied up in the 5 million shares of Enron stock he had used as collateral to obtain loans for personal investments. At the beginning of 2001, Lay owed creditors $95 million for assets purchased against his Enron stock. As Enron's stock declined, he had to pay the margin calls or start selling his assets—such as his three $1 million homes in Aspen, Colorado—to make the calls. Lay needed Skilling to drive Enron's stock price up.[271]

Enron, of course, faced the same margin call predicament. Ninety-seven percent of the financial value of many SPEs consisted of Enron stock. When the financial value of Enron's stock declined, so did the financial value of the SPE, making it difficult for the SPE to meet its loan payments. When that happened, Enron either had to put additional stock into the SPE, which further diluted Enron's stock value, or the SPE had to pay off its excess financial obligations.

In order to attract outsiders to invest the required 3 percent equity in his network of SPEs, Fastow signed agreements in which the outside investors would be paid first should Enron's stock fall below a certain price, or "trigger." The Osprey SPE, which supported the Whitewing SPE, had a $59.78 trigger price.[272] If Enron's stock price went below this amount for several consecutive days, Enron would have to reimburse Osprey's outside investors with Enron stock. Otherwise, the investors could divest from Osprey. Without sufficient outside investors, Osprey's debt would have to be consolidated on Enron's balance sheets, worsening Enron's debt-to-equity ratio. Worried investors would then dump their Enron stock on the market, driving its price even lower, which would set off triggers associated with other Fastow-created SPEs.

Enron's collapse could happen very quickly, unless Skilling and Fastow found ways to drive up the stock price. Given the company's already tenuous economic foundation, the last thing Skilling wanted was for Enron's questionable operations to come under greater public scrutiny. Fastow was more than eager to help, hoping Skilling would reward his good performance by promoting him to the vacant COO position.[273]

More Public Scrutiny: February and March 2001

In 2001, a small handful of stock market analysts started comparing Enron's financial performance to investment banks, rather than energy companies, because Enron had evolved into a trading company. Merrill Lynch's and Goldman Sachs's stock prices were fourteen times their projected earnings. Enron's stock price was forty-four times its projected earnings. Either the investment banks were significantly undervalued, or Enron was significantly overvalued.

A prominent research firm concluded that Enron's $73 stock price was overvalued by about $20.[274] At the annual

"Bears in Hibernation" conference attended by short-sellers—brokers who place bets that a stock will decline in value—James Chanos, president of Kynikos, claimed Enron had evolved into a hedge fund, and a poorly performing, overpriced hedge fund at that. He encouraged others to join him in short-selling Enron's stock.[275]

Other analysts began taking a closer look at Enron's bottom line. During the 1990s, new economy mathematics measured Internet success according to revenue growth. This approach consisted of increasing revenue by achieving greater market share at any cost, driving competitors out of the market, and then cutting costs to become profitable. Analysts shifted their emphasis to profits following the April 2000 dot.com collapse. But they had difficulty understanding Enron's complicated financial statements, including how Enron generated its profits. Investors rely on transparent reporting, and Enron's financial statements were anything but. Some investors began reconsidering whether they should hold Enron stock in their portfolios.

Fortune magazine, which had made business heroes out of Lay, Skilling, and Fastow, took the next shot at Enron by publishing an article disputing Skilling's claim that the company's stock was underpriced.[276] The *Fortune* article opened the door for more critical analysis by other journalists and research analysts. By the end of February, after Skilling's first two weeks as CEO, Enron's stock price dipped below $70, creeping closer to Osprey's $59.78 trigger.

If the analysts needed to see more profits, then Causey and Fastow could provide them. Enron signed a ten-year contract guaranteeing Quaker Oats $4.4 million per year in energy savings and immediately booked $23.4 million of the estimated $36.8 million profits from the contract.[277] Fastow supplemented this with $5 billion worth of SPE-created prepays from J. P. Morgan, Citigroup, and other investment banks.[278] The investment banks were eager to participate because of their high return-on-investments, and some bullying from Fastow. Enron was still in the midst of its mergers and acquisitions buying spree, generating more investment banking fees than any other Fortune 500 company.[279]

Nothing was simple for Enron, not even profits from the California energy crisis. California utilities were unable to pay suppliers, including hundreds of millions of dollars due Enron, because of soaring electricity prices. In addition, the state was preparing to file a price-fixing lawsuit against Enron and other energy companies.[280] When analysts questioned Enron's risk exposure, Skilling noted that its California business, which generated huge profits, was a very small portion of the company's overall operations.[281] Causey used Schedule C revenue reserves to hide $496 million in first-quarter electricity-trading losses. Skilling restructured EES, transferring its financially troubled operations into Enron's much larger wholesale business unit, where its losses could be more easily hidden.[282]

The Broadband Collapse: March and April 2001

Enron's broadband division, EBS, was faring no better. EBS entered the broadband market at the worst possible moment, just prior to the April 2000 dot.com stock market collapse. Broadband users sustained heavy stock market losses, despite Alan Greenspan's attempts to stimulate the economy through Federal Reserve Board interest rate cuts. Investors were cashing out, pocketing their Internet profits, and redirecting their investments to less volatile stocks.

Skilling hoped to ride out the decline, but there seemed to be no end in sight. Even stable, traditional firms reduced their Internet financial commitments. As a result, Enron's bandwidth-trading business revenues dropped from $400 million to $30 million. Enron kept cutting bandwidth prices to maintain its share of a rapidly declining customer base. Competitors were forced to match Enron's lower prices, which led to a 90 percent decline in bandwidth prices, making it nearly impossible for any firm in the industry to earn a profit, including Enron.[283]

Making matters worse, the video-on-demand partnership with Blockbuster had become an expensive black hole. Consumer pilot test results were disheartening. Customers wanted to download the same movies they could rent from the nearby Blockbuster outlet. Instead, their choices were limited to movies produced by the two Hollywood studios that had partnered with Blockbuster. Other movie studios watched, looking to see how royalty and piracy issues were resolved. Enron could not afford the escalating costs, and independently started to explore options for getting their own contractual agreements with other digital movie suppliers.

On March 9, Skilling voided the Blockbuster partnership, incurring a $5 million penalty. The twenty-year agreement ended after only eight months. Meanwhile, Enron had already claimed $53 million in profits from the Blockbuster deal during the fourth quarter of 2000, and another $58 million during the first quarter of 2001.[284] Investors responded negatively to the news, and Enron's stock price dropped 11 percent the following trading day.[285]

A week later word leaked out to the media that EBS would eliminate 250 positions, reducing its employees to 900. Rice, the division's CEO, tried to put a positive spin on the news. He noted that because Enron just completed building its 18,000-mile fiber-optic broadband network many employees were no longer needed, and most would be relocated, rather than laid off.[286] Skilling deflected attention from the Blockbuster failure by announcing a long-term deal with an "on-demand" video game supplier.[287] He claimed that EBS was growing fast, with EBS trades more than double those of the previous quarter. What he failed to mention was that EBS would soon report first-quarter losses of $35 million on just $83 million in revenue.[288]

Investors were becoming increasingly skeptical of Enron pronouncements. Enron's stock price took another beating, declining 8 percent following the lay-off announcement, down to $55.90. Altogether, Enron's stock price declined 30 percent during the first two months of Skilling's reign. As a demonstration of strength, Enron increased its profit expectations for the second time since the year began, this time from $1.70 to $1.75 a share, providing Fastow and Causey with more challenges to meet.[289]

The bad news kept pouring in. Desperate for cash, Enron sold the profitable Portland General Electric, its entryway into the California electricity grid market. Sierra Pacific offered to buy the public utility for $3.1 million, $200,000 more than Enron's purchase price in 1997. However, Sierra Pacific couldn't raise the $2.02 million in cash due to high electricity costs, to which Enron had contributed, and the agreement collapsed.[290] Pacific Gas and Electric, the California utility that owed Enron $570 million, could not pay off its debts and declared bankruptcy.[291]

Complaints by media and research analysts were followed by complaints from Enron lawyers, who wondered about Fastow's SPE dealings, and from Arthur Andersen partners concerned about the financial risks associated with Enron's SPE transactions. The Raptors could not pay off Enron's put options because they were funded with Enron's declining stock, forcing Enron to invest more stock in the Raptors to keep them afloat. Enron sold its $52-a-share stock to the Raptors on credit at a discounted $47 per share. Fastow considered this to be a temporary fix, assuming that Enron's stock price would rise once again, just as it had in the past.[292]

Bass, as a member of Arthur Andersen's powerful PSG, continued to challenge Enron executives. He refused to sign off on the current structure of the Raptors, and instructed Duncan to inform Enron's board of directors about the problem. Duncan, once again, ignored the recommendation from Andersen's Chicago headquarters. Causey complained to senior Andersen partners that Bass was being unfair. He claimed that Bass lacked the creativity Enron needed, and tried to impose his "play by the rules" attitude on Duncan. Back in 1998, Andersen partners had defended Bass on the grounds that a client should not dictate the composition of its accounting team. Bass had transferred to the PSG to reduce his involvement in the Enron account, though he still provided recommendations and criticisms of how the audit was being conducted. Now Causey and other Enron executives requested that Bass be prevented from commenting on Enron transactions from this position as well.

> *DECISION CHOICE.* *If you were a senior Arthur Andersen partner and Enron requested that someone other than Carl Bass from your PSG be assigned to review the audit team's work would you:*
>
> *(1) defend Bass and risk losing the Enron account,*
>
> *(2) request that Bass behave in a more collegial manner with Enron, or*
>
> *(3) remove Bass from the Enron account?*
>
> *Why?*

On Pace to be #1 on the Fortune 500 List: March and April 2001

At Enron's request, Arthur Andersen partners removed Bass from the Enron account and reassigned him to SEC relations.[293] When Bass objected, Andersen's PSG noted he would still be an important advisor on the account, though without Enron's knowledge. With his nemesis removed, Causey could more easily keep the board ignorant of the more than $30 million that Fastow had earned from the LJMs the previous year.[294] The Raptors were restructured and Skilling thanked those who contributed.[295]

More work needed to be done. Causey reduced broadband expenses through several accounting tricks, including doubling the appreciable life of some assets and taking money out of a bonus accrual account.[296] The energy trading and broadband losses, combined with a negative first-quarter cash flow of $464 million, forced Fastow to borrow $1.2 billion for cash, which increased long-term debt to $9.7 billion.[297] Enron's debt payments ballooned to $2.3 million a day.[298]

These events culminated with the release of first-quarter results on April 17. Enron reported very favorable financial news for the first quarter of 2001. Revenue was a whopping $50 billion, more than Enron made during the whole of 1999 and a 281 percent increase compared to the first quarter of 2000. At this pace, research analysts estimated Enron's annual revenue would be $240 billion, enough to replace ExxonMobile as #1 on the Fortune 500. Enron also claimed a 59 percent increase in retail energy services and a sevenfold increase in broadband services delivered. Enron's $425 million in profits beat projected earnings per share estimates by two cents.[299] Based on this good news, Skilling raised Enron's expected annual earnings-per-share target from $1.75 to $1.80. Enron employees were psyched!

But the stress was getting to Skilling. While hyping

Enron's first-quarter results on a conference call with analysts, Skilling lost his patience with a short-seller. Richard
Grubman was no ordinary short-seller. His investment fund
included $2 billion of endowment money from Harvard Uni-
versity, the alma mater of Skilling and other top Enron executives and board members. Grubman criticized Enron's
inability to voluntarily provide balance sheets and cash flow
statements the day of its earnings announcement, as some
companies did. "Well, thank you very much. We appreciate
that [suggestion]. Asshole," Skilling sarcastically replied.[300]

The comment brought cheers from Enron's fraternity-
oriented traders, impressed with Skilling's defense of Enron.
But Skilling was now CEO, not COO. As the company's public face, he had to treat external constituents with greater
respect than the way he treated his own employees. Skilling's
reaction was inappropriate for the person *Worth* magazine
named the second-best corporate executive in the United
States.[301] His comments were widely reported in the business
media, to the dismay of Enron's board of directors who were
more accustomed to the politically savvy Ken Lay. Nonetheless, Enron's stock price climbed back to over $60 a share that
day.

Enron had survived another quarter. Only Skilling,
Causey, Fastow, and some loyal co-conspirators knew about
the financial manipulations associated with meeting quarterly
projections. The other 20,000 or so employees, including Ken
Lay, did not. They believed the hype, which was reinforced by
employee and resource expenditures worthy of a Fortune 10
company competing for the #1 ranking.

Keeping Up Appearances: May and June 2001

Appearances mattered a lot at Enron, and Enron looked
like a thriving company. A constant influx of new employees
joined Enron to pioneer new trading markets as global capi-

talism spread over the world. Traders dealt futures in sugar, coffee, hogs, grains, and meat, among other commodities. Enron would soon begin buying and selling memory chips called "DRAMs," with an estimated market size of $32 billion and infinite potential.[302] Conquering the benchmark 20 percent market share would mean another $6.4 billion in revenue.

Enron was also reshaping the Houston skyline. Employees watched the construction of a $300 million, forty-story tower parallel to their own fifty-story tower. The new tower, scheduled for June 2002 completion, was close enough to be connected with a curved sky bridge.[303] Andy Fastow's wife was busily spending $4 million on art to decorate the building.[304] Meanwhile, Lay purchased a $41 million corporate jet, a state-of-the-art Gulfstream V, to add to Enron's fleet of six jets. He could now fly from New York to Tokyo on one tank of gas.[305] Companies in financial trouble typically did not make these types of extravagant investments.

Everyone, except for a handful of short-sellers, continued to praise Enron. Business ethics professors used Enron as a case study of an innovative company with a social conscience. Well-respected research analysts recommended strong buys on company stock. At luncheon gatherings of energy industry experts, David Fleischer, managing director of Goldman Sachs, predicted Enron's stock would reach $120 a share by the end of the year.[306]

Yet, a mere two-and-a-half months after taking over as CEO, Skilling drafted his resignation letter. Skilling was answerable to the board of directors on a more regular basis and he didn't appreciate their second-guessing. Lay had learned long ago that Skilling did not receive criticism well. Skilling thrived on being an entrepreneur. Becoming a bureaucratic lackey who merely implemented board decisions made work drudgery, not fun. He spoke with Lay about his concerns. When Lay volunteered to intervene with the board of directors on his behalf, Skilling decided not to hand in his resignation letter.[307]

Skilling's dream job was turning into a nightmare. The Dabhol facility and EBS, both filled with initial high-profit expectations, were collapsing. Enron gave up on Dabhol, shutting down the facility in June due to the lack of payment from its sole customer.[308] EBS lost $102 million on just $16 million of revenue during the second quarter, only one-tenth of the sales reported for the same quarter in 2000. Instead of bringing in $5 billion of revenue as predicted, the EBS division lost about $2 billion in less than two years. Skilling merged EBS operations into the wholesale division to enhance efficiency and hide some of its problems.[309]

Rice resigned as CEO of EBS and cashed his stock options. Altogether, he exercised $70 million in stock options during his Enron career, which still paled in comparison to Lou Pai's $250 million.[310] Lay and Skilling were also cashing out. Lay sold $30 million in stock options over the previous six months and Skilling sold $30 million over the previous twelve months.[311]

Dabhol was not Enron's only international problem. Just a few of Enron's $7 billion worth of international assets were profitable, and many others were plagued with cost over-runs.[312] Always thinking big, Enron purchased one of the world's biggest metals-trading companies for $446 million in May 2000. Just one year later, Enron's metal-trading losses exceeded $500 million. As if that weren't bad enough, the London Metal Exchange fined Enron $264 million for breaking trading rules. Enron's official and hidden debt payments escalated.

California's electricity-related problems worsened. Service deteriorated as demand exceeded the very costly supply. Enron was blamed for malfunctioning traffic lights that caused car accidents, passenger elevators that shut down between floors, and computers and ATMs unpredictably turning off.[313] Federal Energy Regulatory Commission officials finally came to California's aid by agreeing to cap electricity prices for a limited time. The bad publicity in California contributed to Enron's stock dropping from $60 in early May to below $50 in mid-June.

On June 21, Skilling arrived in San Francisco to give a speech on energy issues. He believed that state politicians were to blame for the energy crisis. Two weeks earlier, he jokingly compared California to the *Titanic,* a public comment that further wounded Enron's relationship with the state.[314] Protestors wearing pig masks greeted him outside the private club. As Skilling started his speech, a woman ran to the front of the room and threw a raspberry pie in his face.[315] Enron's stock ended the day below $45, wiping out all of the stock market gains made over the past three years.

Vinson & Elkins lawyers successfully hid Fastow's LJM earned income from public documents.[316] But with Enron's stock declining, and rising fears that SPE triggers would be set off, vice-chairman Clifford Baxter, a Skilling confidant, and in-house lawyers expressed concerns about Fastow profiting from transactions between Enron and the LJMs. They added their complaints to those previously raised by Arthur Andersen's Carl Bass, Enron's former treasurer Jeff McMahon, and Enron's research group director Vince Kaminski. Short-sellers continued to educate reporters about Fastow's LJM arrangements, hoping that public knowledge of Fastow's conflicts of interest would further damage Enron's stock price. References to LJM were starting to appear in the media, beginning with a financial investment website in early May.[317]

Skilling concluded that Fastow's dual role as CFO of Enron and managing director of SPEs doing business with Enron had to end before shareholders filed a conflict-of-interest lawsuit. Skilling gave Fastow a choice: remain as CFO and divest from the LJMs or remain an LJM partner and resign from Enron. He could no longer maintain both jobs.[318]

Fastow was tempted to leave Enron for the LJMs and gain the stature associated with being CEO of his own investment fund. The LJMs were the source of his growing fortune, with earnings that would amount to $23 million from his $1 million LJM1 investment and $22 million from his $3.9 million LJM2 investment.[319] On the other hand, Fastow envisioned rising even higher within Enron. He had helped Skilling to succeed and felt worthy of the COO position Skilling had vacated.

> *DECISION CHOICE. If you were Andy Fastow would you:*
>
> *(1) remain Enron's CFO and divest from LJM, or*
>
> *(2) resign from Enron and remain an LJM partner?*
>
> *Why?*

Divesting from the LJMs: June and July 2001

Fastow chose to stay with Enron, sell his financial interests in the LJMs, and find a trusted associate to manage them. The LJMs were still needed to help Enron meet quarterly projections. Without the LJMs, Enron's debt-to-equity ratios looked pathetic. The solution seemed obvious: Michael Kopper, his protégé. Fastow convinced Kopper, already significantly involved in LJM management, to resign from Enron. Fastow and Kopper would remain a team. Their dealings would now appear to be more legitimate to investors and other Enron employees, a win-win for everyone.

Fastow determined his financial interest in the LJMs to be worth $16.35 million. He created a complicated set of transactions that provided Kopper with the necessary cash to buy out Fastow's financial interests. He classified Kopper's resignation as an involuntary termination, which entitled Kopper to a $905,000 severance and an immediate vesting of all his stock options. Kopper earned $10 million on the Chewco closeout and, against the recommendation of in-house lawyers, Enron paid the $2.6 million Kopper owed in taxes on the transaction. In addition, Fastow arranged for Kopper to borrow $15.5 million from Citigroup, one of Enron's largest investment bankers and an LJM investor.[320]

As part of the LJM unraveling, Enron agreed to pay $13.7 million for LJM's interest in an international project that was $200 million over budget, earning LJM a $2.5 million profit. To minimize the appearance of a conflict of interest, the sale would not be made public until after Fastow officially sold his interest in LJM. The sale would take place in July so it would not negatively impact Enron's second-quarter results.[321]

Fastow had other revenue streams in operation for himself and his co-conspirators. The SPE RADR, now owned by

Enron, was still generating cash. In early July, $750,000 from RADR was sent to Kristina Mordaunt, the helpful Enron lawyer who made $1 million the previous year from Southampton.[322]

Fastow's fountain of wealth could only continue if Enron met quarterly projections. Fortunately, Enron's stock inched nearer to $50 a share as the second quarter came to a close. A report of disappointing financial results would reverse the upward trend and cause tremendous financial problems for Enron by setting off more triggers hidden within Fastow's network of SPEs. The Whitewing SPE had a $48.55 trigger price and the Osprey SPE had a second trigger price at $47. Outside investors were guaranteed to be paid with Enron stock to cover their losses if Enron's stock price remained below these prices for several days. This would dilute the value of existing stock, causing Enron's stock to decrease even further.[323]

Skilling Resigns: July and August 2001

Before the end of the second quarter, Fastow needed some quick sales and accounting manipulations. He and Causey booked the $1 billion sale of three power plants as recurring operational earnings, rather than onetime earnings, to prop up Enron's financial statements.[324]

On July 12, Enron announced second-quarter income of $50 billion, almost triple that of the same quarter the previous year. Income from Enron's wholesale services business nearly doubled. Reported earnings for the first six months of 2001 totaled $100 billion, matching the revenue Enron reportedly earned for the entire previous fiscal year.[325] Enron also reported quarterly net income of $404 million. Its earnings per share reached 45 cents, exceeding second-quarter expectations by 3 cents a share, a 32 percent increase from the same quarter the previous year.[326] The day ended with Enron's stock price situated at $49.55, poised for a new burst of energy.

Fortunately, Enron's second-quarter cash flow statements did not have to be publicly released for another few weeks. But the impact remained very real—a negative $1.3 billion, Enron's worst ever quarterly cash flow from operations. Fastow borrowed $1.97 billion to pay the bills.

At $49.55, Enron's stock price was still too close to the SPE trigger prices and too far from the $80 price when Skilling took over back in February. Skilling was accustomed to success, not failure, and his January prediction of $126 a share haunted him. Skilling defined himself according to Enron's stock price, and he began losing faith in his ability to manage the firm. Enron was not the only firm overestimating demand—all growth stocks were in decline—but the hours and financial pressures were getting to Skilling. He was burning out from working early morning to late at night, seven days a week. He had been working full-time since the age of fourteen and needed separation from his all-consuming workload. His inability to do so a few years earlier had cost him his marriage. According to Enron's rumor mill, Skilling was struggling with depression and drinking more than he should. He certainly wasn't having any fun being CEO; he couldn't get to sleep at night.

The day after Enron's second quarterly performance announcement, Skilling told an astonished Ken Lay he wanted to resign.[327] He needed to get away from job stress and end his relationship with Enron. He wanted to spend more time with his three children and new fiancée, a former Andersen accountant who had joined Enron as a risk manager.[328] Skilling didn't set a specific departure date, but wanted out soon. Lay hoped Skilling would change his mind, particularly since Lay had planned on naming him chairman of the board at the end of the year, as Lay himself was already negotiating his own separation from Enron. Now he would have to pass up a lucrative opportunity to serve as an advisor to a leverage buyout firm.[329] Enron had not yet filled the COO position vacated by Skilling back in February. Skilling's departure would leave two huge vacancies, COO and CEO.

Ken Rice, Skilling's good friend and former CEO of EBS, prepared for Skilling's resignation by selling 772,000 shares for a $28 million profit.[330] But outside a very small network of important executives, Skilling's resignation intentions remained a secret.

Enron's stock price began to creep downward, closing at $46.70 on July 23. The stock dropped to $43.20 a share, before settling in at around $45 over the next several days. Then, on August 8, tragedy struck. Three Enron employees died in an explosion at the Teesside facility, and the company's stock dipped below $43.

Skilling diligently met with other executives to make sure that Enron didn't have any unexpected problems brewing. The release of bad financial news when investors learned of his resignation could cause a public relations nightmare.[331] Reporters would link the two events, generating a massive stock sell off. Each executive provided a positive interpretation of Enron's known problems, including Causey. After being assured that all current problems were manageable, Skilling told Lay he would inform Enron's board of directors of his decision at its mid-August meeting.[332]

On Monday, August 13, Skilling notified the board he was resigning due to "family matters." He planned to give up his seat on the board within a week. Skilling told them that his decision did not have anything to do with Enron's future performance, which he considered very favorable, and that he had no other job prospects. As a sign of good faith to the company, Skilling would repay a $2 million loan and forfeit $20 million in severance pay.[333]

Enron conveyed this information to the public the following day, after the stock market closed. Lay informed stunned reporters that Andy Fastow and Richard Causey were among those being considered to replace Skilling.[334]

Lay Learns about Fastow's Raptors: August 2001

On Wednesday, August 15, word of Skilling's sudden departure spread throughout the company. For many employees, Lay's return as CEO was welcomed. Unlike Skilling, Lay's warm personality charmed those he encountered. The board of directors rewarded Lay with what he needed most, a $10 million bonus and more stock options to help pay his margin calls.[335] Lay, exhibiting the personal skills that endeared him to others, announced an all-employee meeting at the nearby Hyatt Regency Hotel on Thursday. He told employees to submit comments and questions for him to address in a suggestion box in the human resources office.

Sherron Watkins, a vice-president who worked for Fastow, had her own understanding of Skilling's unexpected resignation. She had been an Arthur Andersen auditor prior to joining Enron in 1993. She saw many of Enron's major problem areas during her eight years at Enron. Watkins worked with Fastow on the JEDI portfolio before moving on to Mark's international division and Rice's EBS division. After employee layoffs there, she rejoined Fastow's finance group.[336]

Watkins was familiar with the Raptor transactions and assumed Skilling's resignation had something to do with accounting manipulations that artificially inflated revenues. She estimated that the Raptors owed Enron more than $500 million on hedges, money Enron had already claimed as revenue. But the Raptors were short on cash because they were funded primarily with Enron stock, which had declined significantly in value since Skilling became CEO.[337]

Watkins surmised that informing government officials about Fastow and Causey's accounting frauds would lead to a massive sell-off of Enron stock, and destroy the company. Enron's collapse would mean the end of her own lavish lifestyle, as well as that of her colleagues, and she didn't want that to happen. Instead, for the good of the company, she sought to address the problem internally. Although Lay was well known for wanting to hear only good news, she composed an anonymous one-page letter that highlighted some of Fastow's accounting manipulations.

Watkins wrote that "Skilling's abrupt departure will raise suspicions of accounting improprieties and valuation issues...I am incredibly nervous that we will implode in a wave of accounting scandals."[338] She offered several solutions to the accounting problems associated with the Raptor accounts and overvaluation of assets. Watkins recommended that these problems be fixed before a disgruntled employee informed the SEC. She noted that Lay probably could not address the technical details at the all-employee meeting, but suggested that "you give some assurances that you and Causey will sit down and take a good hard objective look at what is going to happen to [the SPEs] in 2002 and 2003."[339] Watkins then inserted the letter in Lay's suggestion box.[340]

> *DECISION CHOICE. If you were Ken Lay would you:*
>
> *(1) respond to the concerns of the letter at the all-employee meeting, or*
>
> *(2) not say anything about these issues at the meeting but investigate them further after the meeting?*
>
> *Why?*

Wall Street Journal Investigation: August 2001

Lay shared the letter with Causey, who advised that the issues raised in the anonymous letter not be directly addressed at the all-employee meeting.[341] Lay agreed.

Skilling's resignation led to a massive selling of Enron stock. On August 15, the first day of trading following the public announcement, more than 29 million shares of stock traded hands, far more than the 2 million shares traded the day prior to Skilling's resignation.[342] Not many people believed that the well-known workaholic would quit his dream job after only six months just for the sake of his family; in particular, investigative business reporters assumed Skilling must be running away from something.

The *Wall Street Journal* assigned two reporters to the Enron case: Rebecca Smith, who covered the energy industry, and John Emshwiller, who wrote about business frauds and other white-collar crime. After contacting several sources, John Emshwiller wondered if Skilling was the mysterious senior officer referred to in company documents who, at the end of July, withdrew from participation in a Special Purpose Entity doing business with Enron. Enron's public relations director informed Emshwiller that the oblique reference was to Fastow, Enron's CFO, information that further increased Emshwiller's curiosity.[343]

The public relations department notified Skilling about the *Wall Street Journal* inquiry, and he personally called Emshwiller to correct any misunderstanding. During the course of their telephone discussion Skilling admitted that the pressure caused by Enron's plummeting stock price bothered him a great deal. Emshwiller now had subject material for a follow-up story, which would give him another day to research the partnerships that did business with Enron. Rumors began to circulate. Merrill Lynch, which participated in several questionable prepay schemes with Enron, lowered Enron's stock rating from "buy" to "neutral."[344] By day's end, Enron's stock dropped 6 percent to $40.25.

On Thursday morning, August 16, more than one thousand employees gathered at the Hyatt Regency and greeted Lay with a standing ovation.[345] He calmed employee fears about the company's operations, including its stock price, and spoke proudly about Enron's ethics. Demonstrating his faith in the company's future, Lay offered every employee stock options worth 5 percent of their salaries that could be vested immediately.[346] Lay encouraged employees to buy additional stock as a sign of faith in Enron. Lay then flew to New York and gave a similar pep talk to financial analysts.

Enron's stock declined another 8 percent during the day, closing at $36.85. Lay, whose investments were funded with Enron stock, sold 3,500 shares for a net gain of $104,740. Whereas he had recommended that employees buy Enron stock, Lay continued to unload some of his stock holdings over several consecutive days, selling a total of 78,500 shares for a $2.1 million profit. Skilling continued selling his stock options as well, for a total of $37 million over the next month.[347]

Lay did not address the assertions made in the anonymous letter at the all-employee meeting.

> *DECISION CHOICE. If you were Sherron Watkins would you:*
>
> *(1) let the matter drop,*
>
> *(2) send another anonymous letter,*
>
> *(3) admit to being the letter's author and ask to meet with Lay to discuss its contents,*
>
> *(4) inform your contacts at Arthur Andersen,*
>
> *(5) inform the SEC, and/or*

(6) confidentially notify the Wall Street Journal?

Why?

Preparing to Meet with Lay about Fastow's Raptors: August 2001

Upset that none of her concerns were addressed at the all-employee meeting, Watkins went to the human resources office to find out whether Lay had read her letter. The human resources vice-president informed Watkins that Lay not only had read the letter but had shared it with several executives, including Fastow, her boss, and Causey.[348] Given the letter's details, it wouldn't take Fastow or Causey long to determine its origin. Watkins gave the human resources vice-president permission to tell Lay that she had authored the letter. The vice-president then scheduled a meeting between Lay and Watkins for the following week.

The next day, Watkins composed a second letter that provided additional details. She showed a draft of the letter to her friend Kristina Mordaunt, Enron's in-house lawyer. Unknown to Watkins, Mordaunt earned $1 million on her $5,800 investment in Fastow's Southampton Place SPE. Mordaunt accused Watkins of trying to destroy the company and insisted that Watkins first meet with another in-house lawyer before sending the letter to Lay.

The second in-house lawyer was already familiar with Watkins's anonymous letter and advised Watkins not to raise the issue again with Lay. He wondered why Watkins questioned the informed decisions of Fastow and Causey, particularly since Arthur Andersen auditors and Vinson & Elkins lawyers had signed off on the SPE transactions. He promised to contact Enron's chief legal counsel about the issues Watkins highlighted.[349]

> <u>*DECISION CHOICE.*</u> *If you were Sherron Watkins would you:*
>
> *(1) cancel your meeting with Lay and wait until hearing back from Enron's in-house lawyers,*

(2) continue your own investigation and meet with Lay at the already scheduled time,

(3) inform your contacts at Arthur Andersen,

(4) inform the SEC, and/or

(5) confidentially notify the Wall Street Journal?

Why?

Meeting with Lay: August 2001

Refusing to be bullied by corporate lawyers, Watkins continued her own personal investigation into the troubled Raptor accounts. On Monday, she found out that Causey had recommended that Lay not address her anonymous letter at the all-employee meeting. Watkins contacted a friend at Arthur Andersen who was not associated with the Enron engagement team for advice on whether she should continue to make an issue out of Fastow's LJM conflicts of interest and the anticipated Raptor problems. He reminded Watkins of her professional obligation to abide by the highest accounting standards. The Arthur Andersen contact sent a memo summarizing his conversation with Watkins to David Duncan, the lead auditor on the Enron account.[350]

Next, Watkins met with Jeff McMahon, a friend who previously had criticized Fastow's involvement in the LJMs to Skilling, only to be reassigned. After reading Watkins' new letter, McMahon recommended that she cancel her half-hour Wednesday meeting with Lay. He argued that the accounting issues were too complicated for Lay to understand. It would end up being her word against Fastow, Causey, the external auditors, the in-house lawyers, and the external lawyers. She didn't have a chance.[351]

Watkins left her meeting with McMahon more committed than ever to inform Lay about the accounting problems others were hiding from him. Lay would have to know about all potential problems, and respond appropriately, for Enron to survive Skilling's resignation. At the very least, Enron would have to restate earnings due to the accounting manipulations, and the sooner the better.[352] That day Lay sold 25,000 shares for a $387,000 profit, and the next day he sold another 68,620 shares for $1 million.[353]

Watkins met with Lay after lunch on Wednesday, August 22. Lay didn't seem to grasp the depth of the accounting problems she described. He put greater credence on the fact that Arthur Andersen auditors and Vinson & Elkins lawyers signed off on them. Lay charmed Watkins to such a degree during their meeting that when he directly asked Watkins if Fastow was doing a good job as CFO, she agreed. Lay also asked Watkins if she had informed anyone outside Enron of her concerns.

> *DECISION CHOICE. If you were Sherron Watkins would you:*
>
> *(1) tell Lay that you informed someone at Arthur Andersen, or*
>
> *(2) lie and say you didn't inform anyone else?*
>
> *Why?*

Responding to Watkins: August 2001

Watkins lied. Lay, ever the congenial politician, ended the meeting by asking how he could best serve Watkins in the present moment. She requested a transfer from Fastow's office to the human resources office and he promised to look into the possibility. Watkins then departed for her summer vacation.[354]

After Watkins left, Lay contacted Enron's legal counsel and requested an investigation of her charges. Contrary to Watkins's advice, Enron hired Vinson & Elkins to conduct the investigation because the firm was already familiar with the SPE transactions. Watkins had argued that doing so would result in lawyers reviewing the work of their colleagues, which would more likely result in a cover-up than in honest disclosure.[355]

Lay instructed the human resources department to determine whether Watkins's concerns were widely held. Human resources staff quickly surveyed Enron employees regarding their concerns about this tumultuous time period. Only a few mentioned the possible accounting problems. On the other hand, several thousand complained about Enron's highly politicized performance review process.[356]

Fastow exploded when he found out that Watkins, his subordinate, not only had authored the anonymous letter but also had met Lay in private to discuss SPE transactions. He demanded that Watkins and her secretary be fired immediately.[357] Fastow went into Watkins' office and confiscated her laptop computer while she was still away on vacation.[358] Enron obtained legal advice from Vinson & Elkins on how to deal with Watkins and found out that Texas laws did not protect so-called whistleblowers. Nonetheless, the lawyers recommended against firing Watkins because the resultant legal fight would be played out in the media to the detriment of Enron's already ailing stock price.[359]

Lay probably learned more about the inner workings of

Enron over the last two weeks of August than he had during his previous fifteen years as CEO. Enron executives provided daily briefs about the company's organizational problems, including accounting manipulations that took place during his previous command stint as CEO. The most urgent problem was financial—what to do about the billions of dollars in losses hidden by overvalued assets and SPE balance sheets. Officially, Enron had $12.8 billion of debt. But now Lay and the board knew the real total was nearly three times that amount, around $35 billion. Enron's debt had increased more than 60 percent over the past twelve months.[360]

After the first two quarters, Enron had claimed more than $100 billion in revenue, bringing the company in direct competition with ExxonMobile and General Electric for the world's largest corporation. What would happen to Enron's stock price if the public found out that the company had $7 billion in losses?[361]

Fortunately, it was still August. The third-quarter books wouldn't close until the end of September, and third-quarter earnings wouldn't have to be released publicly until the middle of October. Lay met frequently with Causey, Fastow, and other executives to discuss Enron's future.[362]

> *DECISION CHOICE. If you were Ken Lay would you:*
>
> *(1) restructure Enron,*
>
> *(2) merge with another firm, and/or*
>
> *(3) sell off Enron's crown jewels—the brick-and-mortar pipelines Skilling had long ignored—to pay for some of the debt?*
>
> *Why?*

Public Reaction to Fastow's SPEs: August and September 2001

As Lay and other senior executives debated these options, the *Wall Street Journal*, the investment community's paper of record, informed the entire world about Andy Fastow's SPEs.

The *Wall Street Journal's* "Heard on the Street" column provides substance to the latest rumors. On August 28, the topic was Enron. After reviewing the reasons for Skilling's resignation and Enron's stock slide, Smith and Emshwiller questioned Fastow's SPE dealings: "In another bow to criticism, Chief Financial Officer Andrew Fastow, as of July 31, quietly ended his ownership and management ties with certain limited partnerships. Over the past two years, Enron has placed billions of dollars of assets and millions of shares of its stock into complex transactions with these partnerships."

In addition, they wrote, Fastow "stood to gain if [Enron] lost in the transactions."[363] The Securities and Exchange Commission (SEC) soon initiated an informal investigation of these transactions.[364] The distinction between an informal and formal investigation is important. In an informal investigation, the SEC collects information to determine if sufficient evidence exists for a formal investigation. Stockholders are much more likely to dump stock when the investigation takes on a formal status.

Later that day, Smith received a confidential phone call in reaction to her co-authored *Wall Street Journal* article. The informant noted that Fastow earned more money by managing the LJMs than by being CFO of Enron. This was just the tip of the iceberg—there was a major scandal waiting to be revealed. The informant named names and supplied documents.[365]

That same day, the investment world also learned that two Enron employees had been promoted to important leadership positions. Enron's new COO would be Greg Whalley, who had earned Lay's respect as COO of Enron Wholesale Services. During the first six months of 2001, Enron Wholesale Services traders accounted for $97 billion of Enron's reported $100.2 billion revenue. Enron had become a trading company. Whalley had previously ignored warnings from Kaminski and others about Fastow's schemes, something he could no longer do.[366] Mark Frevert, the current chairman and CEO of Enron Wholesale Services, was promoted to vice-chairman of Enron.[367] The board of directors extended Lay's CEO contract to 2005. Most people assumed Lay would groom Whalley to succeed him.[368]

Neither Fastow nor Causey, who had been previously mentioned as candidates, were promoted. Nonetheless, Lay needed Fastow more than ever because Fastow knew more than anyone else about Enron's finances. Even Sherron Watkins, whom Lay directly questioned about Fastow's over-all performance, belied her true feelings by claiming that Fastow was a good CFO. Lay rewarded Fastow with a renegotiated two-year contract. His new salary, bonuses, and stock options were worth $5.8 million a year. Fastow's contract also stipulated $2.35 million a year in severance pay if he was dismissed prior to March 2005.[369] By the end of the week Enron's stock had dropped to $35, a decline of 8 percent since the *Wall Street Journal* article and more than 22 percent since Skilling had announced his resignation.

The damage escalated at Enron and Arthur Andersen. David Duncan faced criticism from several directions for his accounting of Enron's Raptors transactions. In addition to concerns raised by Carl Bass and Andersen's PSG, Duncan fielded questions from *Wall Street Journal* reporters, Vinson & Elkins lawyers conducting Enron's internal investigation, and the Andersen partner who had read Watkins's letters to Lay.

Duncan reversed his earlier decision and informed Fastow and Causey that the accounting for the Raptors failed to

meet Generally Accepted Accounting Principles. Enron would
have to restate its earnings for the third quarter to reflect the
$1.2 billion accounting mistake made back in December.[370]
Fastow, fearing an investigation, ordered Kopper to destroy
his laptop and any office or home computer files that contained damaging information about the LJMs.[371]

Then another unexpected catastrophe occurred. On September 11, a terrorist attack on the World Trade Towers and
the Pentagon, killing more than three thousand people. The
stock market halted trading. Enron's towers were evacuated as
a precaution against a similar attack in Houston. The nation
went into shock and mourning. Most analysts predicted a negative effect on stocks.

The credit market tightened at the worst time possible,
just when people were beginning to question Enron's credit-
worthiness. Suddenly there were no buyers for Enron's commercial paper, the short-term loans companies rely on to meet
daily expenses. Without informing Lay or the board of the crisis, Fastow and Glisan explored borrowing from Enron's guaranteed line of credit. Fortunately, the credit market improved
the following day and commercial paper buyers were located.
In the midst of this financial crisis, Enron paid Kopper $2.6
million to cover a tax payment related to the Chewco buyout,
money he then funneled to Fastow.[372]

Preparing to Announce Third-Quarter Results: September and October 2001

As soon as the market reopened, the now-departed
Skilling sold another 500,000 shares of Enron stock for $15.6
million, raising his total stock sales since April to $62.6 mil-
lion.[373] A few days later, on September 25, Fastow dissolved
the problematic, yet personally profitable, Raptor accounts.

The accountants closed Enron's third-quarter books at
the end of September and prepared for the October 16 public

reporting of third-quarter financial results. Enron's stock sat at a dangerously low $27.20 a share. Lay, Whalley, Causey, and Fastow had just two weeks to decide the extent of Enron's public confession, although the formal filing of quarterly financial statements to the SEC was not required until mid-November.

Enron employees remained in the dark about the company's true financial situation. Many of them never met Fastow and were fond of Lay. They assumed Lay would never permit the deeds suggested in hostile media reports. Lay conducted online employee forums, where he encouraged employees to follow his lead in purchasing Enron stock at the current bargain prices. Indeed, Lay did purchase $4 million of Enron stock; simultaneously, he sold $24 million of stock to cover his personal expenses.[374]

October began with good news. Enron sold some natural gas assets in India for $388 million, though there was still no buyer for its $3 billion Dabhol power plant. Upper management reached an agreement for Northwest Natural Gas to buy Portland General for $1.55 billion in cash and $270 million in stock. Northwest Natural Gas also took on $1.1 billion in Portland General debt.[375] Enron's stock price started to rise and then leveled off in the low to mid-thirties.

However, the broadband division had an $80 million loss on only $4 million in revenue.[376] Quarterly projections could only be met with the help of $84 million in mark-to-market profits. Total sales for the year would be announced at $138 billion, more than annual sales in 2000, but nowhere near the early 2001 projections. On top of all this, cash flow from operations was a negative $753 million.

Lay had grappled with many crises. He now faced two more: restating earnings due to $1.2 billion in uncollectible Raptor hedges, and informing investors that Enron had $7 billion worth of losses hidden by SPE transactions. Wall Street demanded greater financial transparency. But the company would collapse if the severity of Enron's accounting manipulations became public knowledge. Enron's debt-to-equity ratio would soar, forcing credit agencies to downgrade Enron's debt ratings. The SEC would formally investigate, leading to a massive stock dumping. Enron's stock price could disintegrate further, triggering more debt payments it could not pay. The company could be bankrupt, all within a few weeks.

Fastow and Causey had already hidden $7 billion worth of losses from investors. Lay now faced a decision that would directly impact all 20,000 employees—how honest should he be? Wall Street analysts assumed Enron had undeclared losses of about $2 billion. Lay sought counsel from his executive team. Whalley wanted to begin his term of office with a clean slate by charging as much as possible to the Skilling regime. Other executives felt confident that Enron could reasonably explain losses totaling $1.2 billion. The stock price would decline, but the company wouldn't be destroyed, as would happen if $7 billion in losses were unexpectedly announced. Enron would then have another three months to improve operating revenues before acknowledging additional hidden loses.[377]

> *DECISION CHOICE. If you were Ken Lay would you announce:*
>
> *(1) $7 billion in losses and risk financial collapse,*
>
> *(2) $2 billion in losses to match Wall Street expectations, or*
>
> *(3) $1.2 billion as recommended by some executives?*
>
> *Why?*

Restating Earnings: September and October 2001

Arthur Andersen found itself in a bind. Andersen was already under a cease and desist order from the SEC for its role in a previous accounting fraud. Waste Management, the giant trash-removal firm, had overstated pretax income by $1 billion between 1992 and 1996. At the time, Andersen auditors detected the accounting errors and informed senior managers at Waste Management and Arthur Andersen. Yet, even though the errors were not immediately corrected, the auditors certified the audits. Their negligence was compounded by allowing Waste Management to write off the errors over a ten-year period, a clear violation of GAAP. The problem became public in 1998 when Waste Management restated its earnings by $1.7 billion, then the largest restatement in corporate history. Andersen had violated the public trust.

During the drawn-out Waste Management investigation, Andersen auditors were found to have approved fraudulent financial statements for several other high-profile corporate clients. In June 2001, the SEC had fined Andersen $7 million, the largest fine in SEC history, for its behavior on the Waste Management audit. Four Andersen partners had their CPA licenses revoked for periods ranging from one to five years. In addition, the SEC threatened to disbar Andersen from practicing public accounting if it did not cease and desist from any other fraudulent activities.[378] The government threatened to financially ruin the company if Andersen knowingly approved fraudulent accounting again. A mere four months later Andersen realized it had been fraudulently certifying the books of another client—Enron.

Causey argued against Duncan's desire to restate Enron's earnings by $1.2 billion. A restatement would mean Enron continually made huge accounting mistakes. Already scared investors, expecting the worst, would quickly dump

Enron stock at a time the firm could not afford it; the SEC would investigate, and shareholders would sue. Andersen didn't want an SEC investigation either. Rather than restate its previously certified earnings, Enron could declare "nonrecurring" write-offs totaling $1.01 billion, consisting of $544 million for the Raptor transactions, $287 million for overvaluing Azurix assets, and $180 million for restructuring the broadband division.[379] Duncan argued that the write-offs should be classified as "recurring" losses, rather than onetime nonrecurring losses, and forwarded information to Andersen's legal department for their review.

> *DECISION CHOICE. If you were David Duncan, the lead auditor for a company working under a cease and desist order from the SEC, would you:*
>
> *(1) ignore Enron's objections and restate previous earnings by $1.2 billion, which would likely result in a formal SEC investigation,*
>
> *(2) develop a compromise with Enron and declare* recurring *losses totaling $1.01 million, or*
>
> *(3) accept Enron's desire to declare* nonrecurring *losses totaling $1.01 million, which is the least likely to result in a formal SEC investigation.*
>
> *Why?*

Andersen's Documentation and Retention Policy: October 2001

Duncan agreed with Causey's plan to declare nonrecurring losses and not restate earnings. But Enron would have to issue a separate announcement regarding the $1.2 billion reduction in shareholder equity associated with the accounting error at the end of 2000. Lay and Causey kept Andersen auditors in the dark about the billions of dollars in other overvalued assets and hidden losses.[380]

Duncan insisted that other upper-level Andersen managers review Enron's accounting problems. This meant the involvement of Arthur Andersen's powerful PSG committee. Bass, no longer directly responsible for the Enron account, was aghast to discover that Duncan had misrepresented his previous advice to Enron, which, if adopted back in December, would have minimized the problem. Bass took it upon himself to begin documenting all the mistakes made on the Enron account.[381]

Nancy Temple, Andersen's in-house lawyer, was among those creating a paper trail documenting Andersen's concerns about the Enron audit. In early October she had concluded that an SEC investigation was highly probable, which could put the entire Andersen firm at financial risk for violating the Waste Management cease and desist order.

In the Waste Management case, federal prosecutors used internal documents to make their case, some of which were extraneous memos that could have been destroyed according to Andersen's document retention and destruction policy. While reviewing background material for the Enron audit, Temple noticed that some memos from Bass's PSG committee meetings raised objections about accounting techniques used for the Raptors.[382] Temple did not want a repetition of Waste Management events. On October 12, she sent an email to Michael Odom, the director of Andersen's Houston office, reminding him about Andersen's "documentation retention and destruction policy."[383]

According to the policy, all nonessential audit materials could be destroyed prior to the initiation of formal litigation. Nothing could be destroyed after the SEC announced a formal investigation. The SEC was likely to begin a formal investigation if Enron restated its previous financial statements. Since Enron would be declaring a nonrecurring loss, which rarely led to a formal SEC investigation, it would be appropriate to implement Andersen's document retention and destruction policy. Odom forwarded the email to Duncan for his consideration.

Managing relationships with credit-rating agencies became a high priority item on Lay's agenda. Credit-rating agencies evaluate the quality of a company's publicly traded debt, namely its bonds and commercial paper. A high rating means low interest rates. Enron's credit rating had long been BBB+, seven notches below the rarified AAA rating, yet comfortably within the recommended investment range. The dreaded junk bond status kicked in below BBB-, which meant Enron could survive dropping two credit-rating levels, but no more.[384] Junk bonds have very high interest rates, and low demand, because there is a high likelihood of default; thus the name—junk. As a company's credit rating approaches junk status, debt payment triggers are set off. Those who previously lent money could demand immediate cash repayment, further increasing the likelihood of default.

Enron didn't want to surprise the credit-rating agencies and research analysts; it wanted both oversight bodies to believe the company was in total control of the situation. Lay held a conference call with credit-rating agencies and told them Enron would present a clear financial picture of company operations when third-quarter results became public. He forewarned them about the onetime $1 billion charge against earnings. Lay also notified them that there would be a $1.2 billion downward adjustment in shareholder equity, which would not affect Enron's ability to pay its debts.[385] Enron executives braced themselves for the official announcement, thinking they had appropriately managed the potential crisis. Key constituents might be disappointed, but not surprised.

They were wrong.

The Third-Quarter Earnings Announcement: October 2001

Early Tuesday morning, October 16, Enron issued a press release reporting its third-quarter earnings. Then Lay conducted a conference call with analysts to explain the results and respond to questions. Lay repeated that revenues for the year were at an all-time high, $137 billion for the first three quarters, and earnings were up 26 percent. Recurring net income was up 35 percent compared to the same quarter the previous year.[386] But then came the bad news: a $618 million third-quarter operating loss and a total of $1.01 billion in non-recurring write-offs.

Lay did not tell the analysts that Enron had understated its losses by several billion to minimize the negative effect on its stock price, or that Andersen auditors believed the nonrecurring losses should have been classified as recurring. Analysts questioned Lay about Enron's troubled international investments. Lay purposely misled investors by stating that Enron's Brazilian power plant was a good asset, even though he knew it was overvalued by $1 billion and Enron's own risk unit had classified it as "troubled."[387]

Lay also mentioned that about one-third of the nonrecurring write-offs resulted from transactions related to LJM2, one of the SPEs that involved Fastow. He further explained that in terminating a hedge, Enron cancelled a promissory note and repurchased 55 million of its own shares, causing a $1.2 billion reduction in shareholder equity.[388] Given the gravity of the financial details contained in the press release, many people, including the lead reporters for the *Wall Street Journal*, did not pick up on Lay's equity reduction statement, which did not appear in the press release. Lay reminded listeners that, of the eighteen analysts covering Enron, thirteen recommended a "strong buy" and none recommended "sell."[389]

Research analysts readjusted their projections downward. Enron employees wondered whether they should sell their stock holdings. In two weeks they would not have access to their 401(k) retirement accounts due to a changeover in pension plan administrators. Of the $2.1 billion in Enron's 401(k) plan, approximately 62 percent consisted of Enron stock.

The employees knew they should have a diversified stock portfolio in their retirement accounts. Traditional pension plans are forbidden by law to have more than 10 percent of their funds in any one company, but the law does not apply to 401(k) retirement plans. Taking advantage of this exemption had previously benefited employees. They overloaded with Enron stock when it outperformed the Standard & Poor's 500 Index for three-and-a half years. In 2000, Enron's stock rose 89 percent while the Standard & Poor's 500 Index declined by 9 percent. On top of that, Enron matched 50 percent of employee stock contributions up to 6 percent of salary in their 401(k) plans.[390]

For several months Enron warned employees that their pension plans would be frozen from October 16 to November 13, when records would be shifted to the new pension plan administrator. On October 4, Enron informed employees that access denial to their 401(k) accounts would not take place until October 29. On October 16, the day third-quarter earnings were made public, Enron's stock actually went up 67 cents, closing at $33.84. Instead of claiming losses now, many employees reasoned, why not hold on to the stock and wait until the price inevitably rose again? After all, Enron employees were still busy making trades and energy deals. Fastow himself had purchased 10,000 shares back in August because the stock's low selling price was such a good deal.[391]

> _DECISION CHOICE._ *If you were an Enron employee with a significant amount of company stock in your 401(k) retirement plan, would you:*
>
> *(1) minimize your losses by selling Enron stock at its current low price, or*
>
> *(2) keep the stock and wait until the stock market recovered and the price rose again?*
>
> *Why?*

Media Frenzy: October 2001

Most Enron employees chose firm loyalty over minimizing their losses. But outside investors began doubting the wisdom of holding Enron stock and by the end of the day more than 8 million shares of Enron stock were traded, twice the normal activity.[392]

Newspaper reporters, government regulators, portfolio managers, research analysts, short-sellers, class-action lawyers, and credit-rating agencies remained busy doing their jobs. Temple was wrong about the SEC. Although Enron did not restate previous financial statements, the nonrecurring losses were substantial enough for the SEC to consider formally opening a case against the company.[393]

On Wednesday, October 17, a disgruntled group of shareholders filed a class-action lawsuit against Enron for insider trading. The lawsuit accused twenty-nine corporate executives and board members of profiting on information not available to the public dating back to January 18, 2000, just prior to the EBS rollout. Lou Pai led the pack at $270.2 million in stock sales, followed by Ken Lay at $184.4 million, and board member Robert Belfer at $111.9 million.[394] The public learned that Enron's entire inner circle had cashed out their options while simultaneously recommending that other employees buy Enron stock for their 401(k) accounts. A copy of the lawsuit was sent to Enron employees to sign on as plaintiffs.

The *Wall Street Journal* investigative journalists set their sights on Fastow's SPEs. Emshwiller and Smith used Enron's earnings press release as an opportunity to question Fastow's LJM partnerships in the newspaper. A short-seller, disappointed in the newspaper's coverage of Enron's third-quarter earnings announcement, complained to Emshwiller that he and Smith failed to inform readers about the $1.2 billion reduction in shareholder equity Lay mentioned during the previous day's conference call.[395]

Emshwiller became suspicious about such key information having been left out of the press release. Smith found out that the accounting mistake was related to a transaction involving one of Fastow's LJM partnerships. This information was relayed in a follow-up newspaper article about Enron's troubles.[396]

The newspaper article generated a telephone call from another short-seller, who faxed Smith a copy of the latest LJM2 quarterly report.[397] The report stated that LJM2 paid approximately $7.5 million in management fees for the year 2000. Another $75 million was distributed to LJM2 partners during the most recent financial quarter. One of the recipients was the CFO of Enron, the company LJM2 did business with.[398] The relationship between Enron and LJM2 looked corrupt and the firm's stock declined nearly 5 percent.

On Friday, October 19, for the third consecutive day, the *Wall Street Journal* published a prominent article critical of Enron, this one under the headline "Enron's CFO's Partnership Had Millions in Profits." The article informed investors that one of Fastow's partnerships earned about $4 million on a $3 million investment, and generated more than $7 million in management fees. The news media jumped on the information, amplifying Enron's problems worldwide.

On Monday, October 22, Enron informed the public that the SEC had initiated an informal inquiry regarding Fastow's partnerships. Fastow's days were numbered.[399] Enron's stock price dropped 21 percent, from $26 to $20.60, during the day, which threatened to set off additional triggers hidden within Fastow's SPEs. Fastow, long considered one of Enron's best assets, had become a major liability. Skilling was no longer around to protect his protégé. Whalley, the new COO, considered Fastow incompetent.

Lay reacted quickly to the increasingly bad news. On Tuesday, October 23, he broadcasted an all-employee meeting worldwide via video and the Internet. He also conducted an emergency conference call with analysts.[400] Lay assured both audiences that Fastow would continue as Enron's CFO. He ardently defended the company's financial stability, even though Enron's only readily available source of liquidity was a $3 billion corporate line of credit. He contacted a rival energy firm about a possible merger to bail out Enron.

The employee group was more congenial than the analysts. Enron listed its debts at $13 billion, but when all the SPEs were taken into consideration Enron's debt amounted to $38 billion.[401] Richard Grubman, the short-seller who had unnerved Skilling back in April, quizzed Lay about the Marlin SPE. Marlin's $1 billion debt would be added to Enron's accounting ledgers if Enron's credit rating reached junk bond status. Lay refused to answer Grubman's question and diverted listeners by informing them that Grubman was profiting from Enron's stock price decline.[402] Other analysts questioned Enron's credibility, demanding an explanation of Fastow's role in the questionable partnerships, a question Lay avoided. The conference call failed miserably. Investors and the media became more concerned. A highly respected analyst at Prudential changed her recommendation for Enron's stock to "sell," the first analyst to do so.[403]

Skilling listened in on the conference call and grew frustrated with Lay's defensiveness. He contacted Lay and lobbied to return as Enron's CEO. He wanted to help the company manage the momentary crisis. Skilling thought his reappearance would restore some of Enron's credibility.

> *DECISION CHOICE. If you were Ken Lay would you:*
>
> *(1) accept Skilling's offer to return as CEO, or*
>
> *(2) reject Skilling's offer?*
>
> *Why?*

Redundant Documents: October 2001

Lay rejected Skilling's offer.[404]

According to Andersen's document retention and destruction policy, Duncan's engagement team had been very lax. Redundant documents should have been removed from the audit after its completion of the 2000 audit earlier in 2001. Andersen's in-house lawyer strongly suggested that the policy be invoked prior to a formal SEC investigation into the Enron account.

> *DECISION CHOICE. If you were David Duncan would you:*
>
> *(1) implement Andersen's document retention and destruction policy, or*
>
> *(2) preserve all Enron documents to assist any future SEC investigation?*
>
> *Why?*

Fastow's Departure: October 2001

Duncan followed Nancy Temple's advice and implemented Andersen's documentation retention and destruction policy before the SEC inquiry took on the status of a formal investigation. On October 23, Andersen employees in the Houston office were directed to start destroying all extraneous documents, emails, and computer files related to the Enron audit. Duncan also deleted Temple's name from a memo involving legal advice on a contentious issue.[405] The policy was also invoked in Andersen's Chicago, Portland, and London offices.[406]

Board members were very upset with the *Wall Street Journal* exposés about Enron and Fastow. Two board members held a conference call with Fastow about the content of the articles. They were shocked to find out that, during the past two years, Fastow had earned $45 million from the LJM accounts, $23 million from LJM1 and $22 million from LJM2.[407] This was in addition to the $33.6 million of Enron stock he sold and $3 million in bonuses.[408] The board had been led to believe Fastow worked only three hours a week on the LJM partnerships. Instead, the board members learned that Fastow worked two to three days a week on them.[409]

Whalley threatened to quit as COO and president of Enron if Lay did not fire Fastow. The two board members similarly concluded that Fastow should be terminated immediately to restore investor confidence.[410]

The following day, Wednesday, October 24, Enron's leading banks informed Glisan that they would not lend any more money while Fastow remained as CFO. Enron had approximately $1.8 billion in short-term commercial paper loans that needed to be renewed to fund daily operations.[411] Glisan relayed the bad news to Fastow, who shared it with Lay. Lay conducted a conference call with Enron's board of directors to discuss his options. During this phone call the entire board learned about Fastow's $45 million in LJM compensation, and voted to terminate Fastow immediately.[412] One week earlier, Enron executives thought they had everything prepared for the quarterly earnings announcement. Now everything was falling apart.

Fastow would not go down without a fight. He threatened to file a $10 million wrongful termination claim against Enron.[413] Fastow bullied Lay as he had previously bullied other employees and investment bankers. The two agreed Fastow would take an undetermined leave of absence rather than resign. Whalley handpicked Jeff McMahon, the former Enron treasurer previously relocated after criticizing Fastow's SPE arrangements, as Enron's new CFO.

The public learned about Fastow's leave of absence on Thursday, October 25. Prior to the October 16 earnings announcement, with Enron's stock trading at $33.17, investors hoped Enron's stock would rebound after the company clarified its accounting problems. Instead, the earnings report and subsequent analyst conference call further muddied important issues. Enron's stock now sold at $16.41, half its former value. Institutional investors were dumping their holdings on the market.

Each year since Skilling took over as COO in 1997, Enron had managed an annual year-end financial "miracle." Huge negative cash flows were transferred into positive cash flows during the last quarter. In 2000, Enron had a negative $547 million cash flow from operations after two quarters. But when the annual books were closed six months later, Enron reported an astounding positive cash flow of $4.7 billion.[414] Now neither Skilling nor Fastow were around to spin their magic.

Lay was on his own and the situation kept getting worse. On Thursday, October 25, while *Wall Street Journal* reporters were investigating the SPE Chewco, which did about $400 million in deals with Enron, moneylenders resisted renewing Enron's commercial paper. Investment banks were caught in the middle. Enron was obviously desperate for money. If they loaned Enron money, they might never get it back. But if they didn't lend Enron more money, then Enron would not be able to pay off the substantial debts it owed them. Enron owed Chase Manhattan Bank $185 million, UBS Warburg $74 million, Credit Suisse First Boston $71 million, and Bear Stearns $69 million, to name a few. If Enron went under, the investment banks would lose those receivables.[415]

> *DECISION CHOICE. If you were an investment bank executive and Enron already owed you substantial sums of money would you:*
>
> *(1) lend Enron more money to maintain its operations, or*
>
> *(2) refuse to lend Enron money due to the increasing likelihood of it going bankrupt?*
>
> *Why?*

Credit Problems: October 2001

Most banks refused to do business with Enron. But Enron already had a line of credit with a group of banks. Enron borrowed the entire $3.3 billion, of which $2.2 billion was used to buy back some short-term loans and the remaining $1.1 billion set aside for cash on hand. In exchange, the banks demanded Enron's most valuable assets as collateral.

Enron executives directed their attention to the agencies that rate the value of a company's publicly traded debt. Analysts projected that Enron still had as much as $9 billion of debt hidden on SPE balance sheets. Standard & Poor's, a premier independent credit-rating agency, downgraded its long-term ratings outlook for Enron from stable to negative but not Enron's current credit rating. If it had, Enron's situation could have become tragic. Enron would have been forced to sell its own stock to pay off guaranteed loans, diluting its stock value even further. Customers would have stopped conducting business with Enron, fearful that Enron would soon be bankrupt, which would more quickly push Enron into bankruptcy.[416]

But Standard & Poor's is not the only credit-rating agency. On Monday, October 29, Moody's lowered Enron's debt rating to a mere two levels above junk bond status. The announcement contributed to a 10 percent drop in Enron's stock price, the tenth consecutive day the stock declined. The following day, rumors of a takeover caused an increase in its stock price.[417]

On October 31, the SEC announced that its informal inquiry into Enron's transactions with Fastow's SPEs would be upgraded to a formal investigation. They gave Enron until November 5 to provide an honest disclosure of its transactions with the LJMs.[418]

Dynegy Merger: October and November 2001

Enron responded to the SEC investigation by giving the dean of the nearby University of Texas law school a seat on its board of directors. His first responsibility: lead an independent internal investigation of the LJM transactions.[419] But that would not help Enron's worsening liquidity problems. Standard & Poor's had lowered Enron's rating to just one notch above junk bond status.

Enron desperately needed help. Lay tried his political skills on Warren E. Buffet, who refused to bail out Enron. General Electric also passed on the opportunity, as did Royal Dutch Shell, GE Capital, the Carlyle Group, a Saudi prince, and several other buyout specialists.[420] Enron's stock sunk lower with each failed overture, closing at $9.70 on Tuesday, November 6, at $9.10 on Wednesday, November 7, and at $8.40 on Thursday, November 8.

Frustrated, Lay privately pleaded for help from Dynegy, a much smaller energy competitor located in Houston that had copied some of Enron's best strategies. Dynegy had $30 billion in revenue in 2000, compared to Enron's $100 billion. Chuck Watson, Dynegy's CEO, consoled Lay when Enron announced Fastow's leave of absence. At a luncheon meeting the same day, Whalley and two other Enron executives met with a different Dynegy executive and proposed merging the two companies.[421] Three days later Watson visited Lay's house to begin working out a possible deal in which Dynegy would keep Enron afloat by buying its already depressed stock.[422] In some ways the cycle seemed poetic. Enron was created when Ken Lay's Houston Natural Gas merged with InterNorth, a company three times its size. Now Enron would be absorbed by Dynegy, one-third Enron's size.

As another intense workweek came to an end, Andersen auditors finally found out the real details surrounding Chewco, the SPE Fastow had created in late 1997 to buy out CalPERS's investment in JEDI. They could no longer conceal its illegal status. When the complex web of SPEs was unraveled, Chewco's outsider equity was revealed to consist of a loan from Barclay and money from Kopper's domestic partner. Some of the funds distributed by the SPE went to Fastow's wife.[423] Even Causey was ignorant of Chewco's complicated arrangements and illegal status.

On Monday, November 5, the *Wall Street Journal* provided details about Kopper's involvement in Chewco, leading investors to speculate about the participation of other current and former Enron executives. Andersen directed Enron to restate earnings accordingly. All of Chewco's debts had to be added to Enron's balance sheets dating back to 1997, turning previously reported profits into losses.[424] Causey continued to insist that Chewco was a legitimate SPE, until the side agreements guaranteeing profits to outside equity partners were uncovered.[425] Andersen felt pressure from the SEC and demanded that the restatement occur as soon as possible. At this point, Enron's stock had declined to $11.20 a share. Enron needed time to adjust to the new set of circumstances, which meant it could not meet the SEC-imposed deadline for appropriately recording LJM transactions.

Then, on November 8, while Dynegy and Enron executives secretly worked out the specifics of their merger, Enron dropped another public bombshell, announcing that, between 1997 and 2001, it had overstated income by $586 million due to accounting errors related to recording SPE transactions. Profits in 1997, Skilling's first year as COO, had been $9 million rather than the reported $105 million.[426] Profits in 2000 had been overstated by $132 million. And for the just completed third quarter of 2001, Enron losses totaled $635 million, not the $618 million initially reported. Enron also admitted that the Raptors provided more than $1 billion in pretax earnings the previous two years.[427] Treasurer Ben Glisan and in-house lawyer Kristina Mordaunt, both of whom had financially benefited from their SPE investments, were fired.[428]

The same day, the SEC subpoenaed Arthur Andersen. Duncan halted the massive shredding activities that had been going on for two weeks. Truckloads of paper records had been shredded. In addition, 30,000 emails and computer files were destroyed. Enron's stock price declined to $8.40 a share. Enron was losing $2 billion a week. Lawsuits from employees and creditors began piling up.[429]

> *DECISION CHOICE. If you were on Dynegy's secret negotiating team would you:*
>
> *(1) continue negotiating but reduce the amount of money you were willing to pay for Enron, or*
>
> *(2) end negotiations before a public announcement might damage Dynegy's own stock?*
>
> *Why?*

Enron Acquired: November 2001

Despite the onslaught of bad news, Dynegy continued negotiating with Enron. Dynegy wanted to acquire Enron's natural gas pipelines and traders. Relief finally came to Enron on Friday, November 9, when Dynegy publicly announced its intentions to acquire the company for $9 billion.[430] The agreement included an immediate cash payment to Enron of $1.5 billion and another $1 billion when the merger was concluded.[431] Dynegy would inherit Enron's $12.8 billion debt. The collateral consisted of InterNorth's original pipelines. If everything else failed, Dynegy would get Enron's pipelines, which Dynegy considered worth the gamble.

There was no doubting who had the upper hand. This was an acquisition by Dynegy, not a merger with Enron. The merged firm would be named "Dynegy." Dynegy would have eleven seats on the new fourteen-member board and own 64 percent of the company.[432] If either party backed out of the agreement it would have to pay the other party a $350 million penalty.[433]

Ken Lay took care of himself during the negotiations. He was entitled to one of the three director seats assigned to Enron.[434] Unknown to the public, he also negotiated a $60.6 million severance package, $20.2 million for each of the three years remaining on his contract. He needed the money to meet his margin calls.

Enron's key traders watched the value of their stock options plummet. The long list of top executives whose stock option sales were documented in the class action lawsuit further angered them. They conveyed their discontent to Whalley and threatened to quit Enron if they were not financially rewarded for staying. These essential employees could make or break the deal because Dynegy wanted them.

Whalley offered seventy-six essential Enron employees an average retention bonus of $1 million in cash. Dynegy balked at such an extravagant payout, and reduced the number

of employees offered retention bonuses from seventy-six to
twenty-five. Enron's top trader received $8 million to stay.[435]

Enron was saved! Some Enron employees began purchasing Enron stock under the assumption that the price
couldn't get any lower than the current $8 a share, given the
quality people still employed by the company.

> *DECISION CHOICE. If you were an Enron
> investor would you:*
>
> *(1) hold onto the shares knowing that Enron's fate
> was bound to improve following the acquisition,
> or*
>
> *(2) sell your shares at $8, take your losses, and
> invest in a more reliable company?*
>
> *Why?*

The Hero Turned Enemy: November 2001

The next Monday, November 12, Enron's credit rating was downgraded to just one level above junk bond status. This created a new crisis because one of Fastow's SPEs had a trigger linked with a BBB- credit rating. Enron had two weeks to pay back the $690 million it borrowed through the SPE.[436] Enron executives were so immersed in solving the problem that they neglected to inform Dynegy.

Ken Lay had long been the hero of company employees, local community groups that benefited from his generosity, and people seeking ways to help the United States end its addiction to coal and oil. Enron employees rallied around his every pronouncement, which included being able to trade on the Enron stock in their 401(k) retirement accounts a week earlier than anticipated. They blamed Fastow and the media, not Lay, for the terrible financial hit they took. On November 13, the first day they could trade, Enron's stock was selling at around $10, down from the $29 closing price on October 19, when some Enron employees mistakenly thought the freeze began, and down from the $15.15 opening price on October 29, when the freeze actually began.[437]

Lay's support evaporated when the media informed the public about his $60.6 million severance agreement with Dynegy. While some employees were in the process of losing their life's savings and expected to lose their jobs, the man ultimately responsible for the company managed to come out with $60.6 million in severance pay. The employees erupted with anger at their former hero.

> *DECISION CHOICE. If you were Ken Lay would you:*
>
> *(1) keep the entire severance package,*
>
> *(2) offer some of the severance package to Enron employees, or*

(3) cancel the severance package?

Why?

Out of Control: November 2001

Lay, always shy of confrontation, responded to the anger by allocating one-third of the severance to a special charitable foundation for Enron employees facing financial hardships. When this did not quell people's anger, Lay boldly forfeited the entire severance agreement.

But even such a magnanimous sacrifice seemed meaningless when compared to the amount of money he had earned from Enron. The *New York Times* reminded readers that, since 1989, Lay had earned $13 million in salary, $26.8 million in cash bonuses, and $266.7 million in stock profits, a total of more than $300 million. While Enron's stock had precipitously declined throughout 2001, Lay earned $20.7 million from his stock options.[438] Lay was selling his stock to meet margin calls, but the media stories failed to mention that.

Lay's challenges multiplied when Enron's new CFO informed him and Dynegy's CEO that Enron had to unexpectedly repay $690 million in loans due to the BBB- credit rating.[439] Enron's accountants estimated that the firm needed another $3 billion to remain solvent until the end of 2002.[440] Lay hoped for a federal bailout similar to the one Chrysler had received three decades earlier, but the nation's political climate had changed. Not even honoring Federal Reserve Chairman Alan Greenspan with the Enron Prize for Distinguished Public Service in the middle of the current crisis gained Enron any federal help.

Enron was bleeding money and drastic action was needed. The company only had $1.2 billion in cash, less than the $1.5 billion cash investment Dynegy had given the company earlier in the month.[441] Lay and other top managers sorted Enron's businesses into one of three categories: definitely keep, definitely sell, and maybe sell. It was time to focus on what Enron did best, which included natural gas pipelines, gas and electricity trading, coal trading, and retail operations. These businesses would be kept. Among the businesses available to the highest bidder were Enron's three biggest headaches: EBS, Dabhol, and Azurix.[442] These sale items came with huge debts.

Enron employees who weren't offered retention bonuses or promises from headhunters hoped to be laid off during the reorganization process. Enron's generous severance package, which would likely be changed during negotiations with Dynegy, entitled employees to one week of pay for each year of service, up to a maximum of six weeks, plus a week's pay for each $10,000 of base salary. This amount could be doubled by signing a statement promising not to sue Enron for the dismissal.[443] A trader employed for two years earning $100,000 base salary who signed the "no legal recourse" statement could receive twenty-four weeks' salary in severance pay, about $46,000, to cover expenses while looking for another job.

On November 19, all eyes were on Enron's quarterly 10Q filing with the SEC, already five days late. The news was terrible. In addition to the unanticipated $690 million in debt due in one week, Enron's debt repayments and other financial obligations through the end of 2002 totaled $9.15 billion. If Enron's credit rating dropped any lower, the company would have to immediately make additional debt payments of $3.9 billion.[444] In addition, Enron restated third-quarter losses by another $29 million, its second restatement in slightly more than one month. Enron was out of control.

Bankrupt: November and December 2001

The extent of Enron's financial problems caught Dynegy executives and stockholders by surprise. Dynegy executives knew that Enron had debts hidden in its SPE network, but they were unaware of the magnitude of the debts because Fastow had hidden them so well. Even more disturbing, Enron accountants were unable to account for the $1.5 million in cash Dynegy had just given Enron.[445] The so-called merger deal was already going through the due diligence process. The sudden bad financial news made Dynegy suspicious about other information Enron had provided for review. After all, Enron declared losses of $618 million on October 16, dismissed its CFO under a cloud of accusations about wrongdoing, needed to use the final $3.3 billion of its credit line to stay afloat, and restated its losses twice, all within a month. In addition, the SEC initiated formal investigations against both Enron and its auditor. Worse, Dynegy stockholders were beginning to bail out as the company's stock dropped from $46.94 to $41.70 in less than a week.[446]

Enron's volatile stock price also made it extremely difficult for Dynegy to determine the economic value of Enron's assets. Initially, Dynegy agreed to exchange 0.2685 shares of Dynegy stock for one share of Enron. By November 23, with Enron's stock in continual decline, Enron's assets losing value due to hidden debts becoming known, and Enron's customers switching to competitors, 0.15 shares of Dynegy stock for one share of Enron seemed to be a more appropriate deal. Dynegy possessed the superior bargaining position and demanded Lay's resignation from the board as part of the acquisition agreement being development.[447]

Dynegy had to work out the details with Enron's lawyers, a large and unruly bunch. Enron employed 145 lawyers at its Houston headquarters, enough to be the sixth-largest law firm in Houston were they a private partnership. Enron's lawyers matched wits with Dynegy's forty-three staff lawyers, and both groups fought to protect their employer's interests.[448]

Enron lost economic value with each passing day. On three consecutive days its stock price, Skilling's ultimate scorecard, dropped below $9, then $7, and then $5. Dynegy informed worried stockholders that it had renegotiated a new purchasing price for Enron—$4 billion—which was less than half the amount agreed to three weeks earlier. Dynegy and Enron pressured the banks to hold off on collecting debt payments from Enron until after the merger became complete in 2002. Otherwise, the deal might collapse.[449]

Then the clock struck midnight. On November 28, credit agencies admitted the obvious—Enron was unable to pay its debts. They reduced Enron's credit rating to the greatly feared junk status. Dynegy immediately pulled out of merger negotiations. The value of Enron's stock dropped from $4.11 to 61 cents as trading volume on the stock zoomed to 345 million shares, compared to the 4 million shares traded on a normal day earlier in the year. The stock of a company that had reported sales of $130 billion and assets worth $62 billion just two months before was now worthless.[450]

Lay, who had risen from rural poverty to the top of the corporate ladder, was now relegated to meeting with bankruptcy lawyers. Together they explored the pros and cons of declaring either Chapter 11 bankruptcy, which protected the company from creditors while reorganizing, or Chapter 7 bankruptcy, an instant liquidation of assets.[451]

> *DECISION CHOICE. If you were Ken Lay would you declare:*
>
> *(1) Chapter 11 bankruptcy and reorganize, or*
>
> *(2) Chapter 7 bankruptcy and put an end to everything?*
>
> *Why?*

Wait for a Phone Call: December 2001 and January 2002

Lay settled on Chapter 11. The company would go on. Keeping the most talented employees on payroll was of primary importance. Otherwise, Enron might as well be liquidated. With headhunters making offers, Enron negotiated from a weak position. Lay and Whalley extended retention bonuses to 500 key employees to help guide Enron through the reorganization process. The final retention agreement totaled $55.7 million for just ninety days of guaranteed services. The payouts included $5 million for the head of trading, $2 million for the creator of Enron Online, and $1.5 million for Jeff McMahon.[452]

Earlier in the year Skilling and others predicted that by the end of December Enron would be #1 on the Fortune 500 list with $240 billion in revenue and a stock price of $126 a share. Instead, Enron, always a record setter, became the largest bankruptcy in U.S. history.

On December 2, having no cash left to pay its bills, Enron temporarily closed its doors to get its house in order. Its 28,500 customers would have to find some other way to meet their energy needs. Enron owed more than $31 billion on assets valued at $49.8 billion.[453] Enron's top three creditors were Citibank, Bank of New York, and Chase Manhattan, with debts ranging from $3 billion to $1.9 billion. Desperate for money, Enron sued Dynegy for $10 billion for breach of contract, a feeble attempt to prevent Dynegy from taking control of the Enron pipeline it received as collateral for the $1.5 billion cash infusion.[454] After all, Dynegy broke the contract only after Enron did to Dynegy what it had done to everyone else since 1991—mislead them about Enron's real financial value.

The following day 4,000 Enron employees received termination notices. Most of them were given thirty minutes to pack their personal possessions and leave the building. They were told to go home and wait for a phone call notifying them if their services would be needed during the reorganization.[455] Adding insult to injury, the Bankruptcy Court cancelled Enron's severance plan and replaced it with flat fee payments of $4,500 per employee, much less than what the employees had anticipated.[456]

On January 16, 2002, Enron was delisted from the New York Stock Exchange. One week later, Lay submitted his resignation. Three days after that, a distraught Cliff Baxter, the former Enron vice-chairman who did not participate in any schemes but had warned Skilling about Fastow's misuse of accounting principles, committed suicide.

Determining Punishments

Enron imploded. Left behind were millions of shareholders owning worthless Enron stock. These owners trusted that Enron executives behaved in the best interests of shareholders and truthfully conveyed financial information in quarterly statements. But that was not the case. The shareholders were betrayed by not only Enron's chairman of the board, CEO, CFO, CAO, and their subordinates, but also auditors, lawyers, and investment bankers who did business with Enron.

Some key players are more culpable than others, a decision that American citizens place in the hands of federal judges and juries. The key players included:

Former Enron CEO and Chairman of the Board Ken Lay: As CEO of Enron from 1985 to 2001, Lay is ultimately responsible for what happens in the company. He did not know of the illegal accounting activities until August 2001, after Skilling resigned. He did not tell the public when he found out about Enron's financial problems.

Former Enron COO and CEO Jeff Skilling: As COO

of Enron from 1997–2001, Skilling relied on Andy Fastow to find creative financial ways to help divisions meet quarterly projections. Several employees complained to him about Fastow's activities and suggested their illegality. After becoming CEO in February 2001, Skilling forced Fastow to step down as general partner of the most contentious SPEs, but did not demand his resignation.

Former Enron Chief Financial Officer Andy Fastow: While working under Skilling in the early 1990s, Fastow created several SPEs that guaranteed profits to investors, in clear violation of generally accepted accounting principles governing SPEs. As CFO in 1999, Fastow created two SPEs where he served as general partner, which earned him management fees and profits totaling $45 million. These two SPEs enabled Enron to hide debt and declare unearned revenue.

Former Enron Chief Accounting Officer Richard Causey: Causey worked closely with Fastow in the creation of SPEs. He showed Fastow how to use loopholes in the law to get around accounting regulations. He benefited from Enron's artificially high stock price, selling stock options worth millions of dollars. He also failed to inform Ken Lay and the board of directors about the accounting scandal until after Skilling resigned.

Former Enron Portfolio Analyst Sherron Watkins: While working under Fastow, Watkins realized that Fastow was engaged in illegal accounting activities. She informed Ken Lay after Skilling resigned in August 2001, when Enron's stock was selling at $43 a share. She did not inform the SEC or the public until after Enron declared bankruptcy on December 2, 2001, when Enron's stock was worthless. In 2002, *Time* magazine declared her "Man of the Year" for blowing the whistle on Enron.

Former Arthur Andersen auditor David Duncan:
Duncan served as Arthur Andersen's lead engagement
partner on the Enron account. He defended Enron's
aggressive accounting techniques and did not convey the
concerns of Andersen's Professional Services Group to
Enron's board of directors. He violated the public trust
placed in auditors and implemented Andersen's documentation retention policy knowing that the SEC would
soon be reviewing all materials related to the Enron
audit.

Merrill Lynch investment bankers: The investment
bankers misled investors about Enron's financial value.
They participated in, and financially benefited from,
prepays and other financial schemes that artificially
inflated Enron's revenue.

> *DECISION CHOICE. If you were a federal judge
> determining punishments for Ken Lay, Jeff
> Skilling, Andy Fastow, Richard Causey, Sherron
> Watkins, David Duncan, and Merrill Lynch
> investment bankers, how long of a jail term would
> you assign to each, after s/he made others finan-
> cially whole again?*

Person	Jail Term	Explain why more or less than other people in chart
Ken Lay, CEO and chairman		
Jeff Skilling, COO and CEO		
Andy Fastow, CFO		
Richard Causey, CAO		
Sherron Watkins, accountant/finance		
David Duncan, Arthur Andersen lead auditor		
Merrill Lynch investment bankers		

PART II

WHAT COULD HAVE BEEN DONE TO MANAGE ETHICAL PERFORMANCE?

It is easy to demonize those involved in the Enron scandal, or to dismiss the scandal as a conspiracy of fools. But if you do, you lose the opportunity for an abject lesson—they are a lot like you and me. Don't let the magnitude of the impact of Enron's decisions obscure the decision itself—whether $7 billion or $100, the size of the numbers shouldn't matter.

Part II explores answers to four critical decision points in the Enron case study: (1) the decision to use aggressive accounting techniques, (2) the decision to act based on loyalty to an unethical boss, (3) the decision to deal with an unethical customer, and (4) the decision to inform the public about financial problems. Aspects of Enron's ethical problems can be found in many organizations. How do you behave when faced with similar business decisions?

This section begins with an honest assessment of ethics at the workplace and provides an ethics decision-making tool that can serve as a moral compass for managers. The decision-making tool is then used to address four critical decision points. The book concludes with the Seven Moral Levees, a framework for systematically minimizing unethical behaviors at work.

An Honest Assessment

What do you call someone who, while reflecting late at night, labels his or her work-related behaviors that day as: ethical, ethical, ethical unethical, ethical, ethical, unethical, unethical, ethical, ethical...? A human being, that's what. What if the unethical behavior was forgetting to attend a meaningless meeting because a sick parent needed medical care? Or the forgotten meeting was very important and the person missed it because he was too busy playing online poker? Or the unethical behavior was lying to investors?

We are all ethically imperfect people. If you disagree, just ask your colleagues, significant other, or your children! Ethical perfection is a goal that is always a few steps into the future, where it remains our entire lives. Saints and sages often describe themselves as being very sinful people. They are fully aware of how far their thoughts and actions are from ethical perfection.

A company is a community of ethically imperfect people that offers many opportunities to behave unethically, through the competition for power and wealth within the organization or in its product market. This is why so many successful executives, when they write memoirs about what they learned during their illustrious careers, conclude that personal integrity is an essential attribute of success.

We are creatures of habit. The more we restrain from acting on our unethical impulses, the easier it is to ignore the next one. The reverse is also true. The more often we act on our unethical impulses, the more difficult it is not to act on the next one.

I have been helping managers to create ethical organizations for more than fifteen years. Managers want to be proud of their organizations. Yet at times they feel pressured to cut ethical corners for the good of the organization. These unfortunate short-term solutions, if publicly known, could significantly damage their careers as well as the organization's reputation.

It takes years to build a solid reputation and only a brief moment to destroy it. The goodwill developed through high-integrity performance can evaporate instantaneously. Common rationalizations for unethical behavior, such as "I was only doing what needed to be done" and "I did it for the good of the organization," sound hollow and self-serving in the glare of the media spotlight.

Ken Lay attributed his genuine kindness and sense of peace and security to his parents. Omer and Ruth Lay sacrificed a lot for their children. Omer moved the family to Columbia, Missouri, far away from his own roots, to provide his children what they needed for future success, a college education. Living for the sake of others is among the noblest of virtues. Doing so entails self-sacrifice. The one thing that should not be sacrificed is ethics. Sacrificing ethics for a short-term goal creates distrust that can lead to ruin. A parent who finds out that a beloved child has lied begins to doubt the information conveyed by the child from that point on. If not confronted, a child's small lie typically leads to bigger lies. Soon the situation may spin out of control, resulting in more severe misbehaviors and punishments.

Lay, Jeff Skilling, and Andy Fastow achieved tremendous financial and hierarchical success during their professional careers. Lay, born into poverty, rose to be CEO and chairman of the board of the world's largest energy company. During the years leading up to Enron's bankruptcy, he earned more than $200 million in salary, bonuses, and exercised stock options, and in early 2001 he owned an additional $350 million in stock options.[457] Skilling advanced from a precocious teenager managing a local cable television program to a Harvard MBA and CEO of Enron. In 2000, he received a $7.5 million performance bonus and between May 2000 and October 2001 he cashed out more than $70 million in stock options.[458] Fastow's career path took him from a finance position in a bank to CFO of Enron. He made more than $60 million from his two LJM investments.[459] These three executives lost all or most of their power and wealth because they did not restrain their pursuit of self-interest when making important decisions that affected others.

Enron's collapse was not inevitable, nor did it happen overnight. As early as 1992, Enron executives began manipulating financial statements. At any point during the next nine years, Enron's misdirected course could have been corrected. But no one stepped forward. The company eventually drowned in a corporate culture flooded by unethical behaviors.

If a boat sailing from New York City to Africa veers northward off course ten miles east of New York City, sailors wisely change course immediately rather than waiting until they've docked in Greenland. Unethical behaviors have to be challenged immediately, otherwise the organization will sail in a dangerously off-course direction. Managers need a moral compass to guide their behavior.

A Moral Compass

How should employees infuse moral reasoning in the process of making business decisions? Ethical reasoning is just like any other managerial problem-solving process. When confronting a problem, managers typically list the available options and determine which of the alternatives makes the most sense. Often, the reasons that support one option are better than the reasons that support others. The same decision-making process can be applied to ethical reasoning.

Social philosophers have determined that some ethical reasons are more morally acceptable than others. For example, it has been long established that "doing to others as you would want done to you" should take precedence over an individual's self-interests when these two ethical theories are in conflict.

The ethics decision-making framework below can help managers reach a moral conclusion regarding the rightness or wrongness of any decision.[460] It provides a moral compass based on six questions that can be applied to any business problem.

An Ethics Decision-Making Framework

Instructions: Answer Questions 1 through 6 to gather the information necessary for performing an ethical analysis. Based on this information, develop a decision that has the strongest ethical basis.

1. Who are all the people affected by the action?

2. Is the action beneficial to me?

3. Is the action supported by my social group?

4. Is the action supported by national laws?

5. Is the action for the greatest good of the greatest number of people affected by it?

6. Are the motives behind the action based on truthfulness and respect/integrity toward each stakeholder?

- If answers to Questions 2 through 6 are all "yes," then do it.

- If answers to Questions 2 through 6 are all "no," then do not do it.

- If answers to Questions 2 through 6 are mixed, then modify your decision.

    - *If answers to Questions 5 and 6 are "yes,"* this action is the *most* ethical. You may need to modify this decision in consideration of any "no" answer to Questions 2 through 4.

    - *If answers to Questions 5 and 6 are "no,"* this action is the *least* ethical. Modify this decision in consideration of these objections.

- *If answers to Questions 5 and 6 are mixed,* this action is *moderately* ethical. Modify this decision in considerations of objections raised by Questions 5 or 6. You may need to further modify this decision in consideration of any "no" answer to Questions 2 through 4.

The answer to the first question provides the decision-maker with a list of people whose interests should be considered when formulating an ethical response to a problem. A clearly ethical action is one that benefits you and your social group, is legal, benefits the majority of people affected by it, and is based on truthfulness and respect/integrity toward each stakeholder. That is a "no-brainer." A similar no-brainer is the unethical nature of an action that harms you and your social group, is illegal, is detrimental to the majority of the affected people, and is disrespectful of everyone involved.

A common ethical dilemma in business arises when an action benefits you and/or your organization but is detrimental to the majority of the affected people or violates someone's rights, such as unsafe working conditions or environmental pollution. These are the types of ethical dilemmas that keep managers awake late at night, provide fodder for newspaper reporters, and resulted in the destruction of Enron. The creative challenge for managers is to determine how to respect the rights and interests of every stakeholder in a way that is beneficial to the organization and its employees.

So, how would a manager concerned about ethics respond to some of the key problems that occurred at Enron?

Determining Economic Value

The first critical incident for the Lay-Skilling executive team occurred during Skilling's initial year as an Enron executive. Skilling honed in on mark-to-market accounting as a possible method for increasing the economic value of the Gas

Bank's performance. He believed that Enron's traditional oil-and-gas pipeline accounting methods underestimated the economic value of the billion-dollar long-term energy contracts his employees signed with utility companies by ignoring the guaranteed long-term future revenue stream. Skilling proposed that the Gas Bank account for the entire value of the contract immediately and make quarterly adjustments based on market changes. Trading companies were allowed to use mark-to-market accounting to determine the economic value of an asset, so why shouldn't the Gas Bank division do so?

This is the decision Skilling faced in the section titled "Mark-to-Market Accounting: 1991 and 1992." Skilling could keep the traditional oil-and-gas accounting system, or he could submit a proposal to the SEC requesting permission to adopt a mark-to-market accounting system for the Gas Bank.

Applying the Six Ethical Questions. (1) The primary stakeholders in this particular situation include Skilling, his Gas Bank division, Enron, and investors. (2) Mark-to-market accounting methods would definitely benefit Skilling. His annual performance bonus was based on the amount of revenue generated by his division. In addition, he was entitled to a $10 million cash bonus when the Gas Bank division's valuation exceeded $200 million and another $17 million when it exceeded $400 million. (3) Skilling discussed the matter with members of his social group, notably Ken Lay and Enron's board of directors, and they supported the accounting change. (4) At the time, doing so was not legal, which is why Skilling sought a special ruling from the SEC.

(5) Mark-to-market had previously not been applied to the natural gas industry because it distorted market analysis, attracting funds that could have been invested in more efficient business operations. (6) Although Skilling said otherwise, the manner in which he planned to use mark-to-market accounting techniques would deceive investors by misrepresenting the actual economic value of his Gas Bank's transactions. Revenue promised, but not yet received, would be

mixed in with revenue actually received.

Based on these answers to the six ethical framework questions, Skilling should continue to use the traditional oil-and-gas accounting system, and look for a more honorable method to determine the economic value of Enron's Gas Bank. This was the SEC's initial conclusion. It refused to change the rule for Enron because it was too difficult to determine the actual economic value of Gas Bank assets using mark-to-market and the method would be prone to manipulative estimations. This would mislead investors, those stakeholders whose interests the SEC had a special duty to represent.

Skilling persevered without major objections from Enron's executive team or board of directors. He obtained a written opinion from another prominent social group—the Arthur Andersen auditors—which promised to closely monitor Enron's accounting for assets under mark-to-market, thus limiting opportunities for deception. With this additional input, and heavy lobbying by Enron, the SEC reversed its initial ruling and granted Enron's Gas Bank division the permission it needed to apply mark-to-market accounting techniques, beginning in 1992.

However, Skilling illegally applied mark-to-market retroactively for 1991 and later used mark-to-market accounting in operational areas not approved by the SEC. Skilling not only violated the law based on his own self-interests, he knowingly misled investors and created inefficiencies in the stock market because competitors were being unfairly measured against Enron's inflated revenues. Once again, there were no major objections from Enron's executive team or board of directors.

In retrospect, a decision that benefited Enron's Gas Bank division in the short term had major negative long-term ramifications for its employees. Surpassing the previous year's inflated revenues became very difficult. The situation escalated into Fastow designing a complex network of SPEs to hide debt and illegally report revenue. The situation worsened with each passing quarter and, nine years later, destroyed the company.

Loyalty to an Unethical Boss

Enron's performance appraisals were skewed toward dealmaking and increasing revenue, not profits or ethics. Skilling's subordinates, as well as employees working in other business units, such as Rebecca Mark, focused on generating high-priced deals, some of which were not profitable. Temper tantrums and unethical behaviors were tolerated from belligerent bullies who brought in large amounts of revenue.

Ken Lay did not change this dysfunctional incentive system because it was aligned with what Wall Street rewarded—revenue growth. Investors were willing to accept financial losses as long as Enron increased market share, with the understanding that profits would come later, when the biggest players in the market dictated prices. Enron's scoreboard was not balanced. Revenue numbers overwhelmed concern about product quality, customer satisfaction, or employee satisfaction.

The process for determining merit raises and promotions is just as important as what is being measured. Skilling created a Performance Review Committee composed of loyalists who gave preferential evaluations to employees who helped other loyalists achieve their financial goals. One negative evaluation from a Skillingite could undo a host of favorable comments from others. As a result, it took an act of heroism for an Enron employee to question any of the deals being made by Skilling's subordinates.

Skilling inserted loyalists in key executive positions throughout the company, and his subordinates did likewise. The fulfillment of small unethical favors leads to requests for even larger unethical favors. During the mid-1990s, Fastow observed outsider investors profiting nicely from his intricate network of SPEs. Fastow wanted some of the profits for himself, but he couldn't invest in a new SPE because, according to Enron's Code of Ethics, senior executives could not invest in a company doing business with Enron. Instead, he requested that Michael Kopper, his assistant and protégé, invest in a new SPE with the intent of funneling a good portion of his profits to Fastow.

This is the decision Kopper faced at the end of the section titled "Entering California's Electricity Market: 1996 and 1997." Kopper could support the plan, oppose the plan, inform Lay about the scheme, notify the auditors, and/or notify the SEC.

Applying the Six Ethical Questions. (1) The primary stakeholders in this particular situation include Kopper, Fastow, Enron, and investors. (2) It was in Kopper's self-interest to support Fastow's plan. He would be praised by his direct boss and receive a favorable performance evaluation that could result in a merit raise, a likely promotion, and a well-endowed personal stock portfolio. (3) Kopper did not inform his peers because Enron's Code of Ethics considered such conflicts of interest unprofessional behavior. (4) All employees are expected to act in the best interest of their employers, to do otherwise would violate foundational legal obligations.

(5) Furthermore, the SPE would continue to hide debt and inflate revenue, thus misleading stockholders about the actual economic value of company operations. (6) Informing Lay, the auditors, or the SEC would be the truthful thing to do.

Based on these answers to the six ethical framework questions, Kopper should oppose the plan. The creative challenge is to oppose it in a way that would not result in losing his job, which is likely to happen if he approached Fastow directly. Kopper is Fastow's friend as well as protégé. Friendship demands that Kopper try to direct Fastow away from illegal schemes before Fastow is caught and fired or arrested. If the friendship is deep, Fastow might be impressed that Kopper is willing to risk being a victim of his temper tantrum over this issue. At the same time, this strategy might not work because Fastow is being guided by emotions, not rationality.

In situations like this, it is useful to reflect on other people who can influence the person whose behavior needs to be changed. Ideally, it should be someone who is respected by the unethical person. The top two candidates in this particular case are Lea Fastow, Andy's wife, and Skilling. Kopper occasionally dined with Andy and Lea. Kopper could meet with Lea separately and inform her of the damage her husband's plans could cause Enron and her husband's career. Lea might be able to convince her husband that the SPE investment is not a wise decision.

Skilling is probably not a good choice because he failed to make any changes when other employees informed him about Fastow's questionable activities. But this might provide the additional information he needed to make the necessary ethical decision.

If neither Lea nor Skilling are viable options, there might be another executive at Enron who has both Fastow's respect and high moral standing. If so, that person should be informed. If not, Kopper has a moral obligation to inform Lay. Informing people outside the company, such as the SEC or media, should occur only after internal decision-makers have been notified and then failed to make the necessary changes.

Sherron Watkins faced a similar dilemma. She worked for Fastow and, as a former Arthur Andersen accountant, had a very good understanding of the financial numbers. In August 2001, shortly after Skilling unexpectedly resigned from his dream job, Watkins sought to address the problem internally by submitting an anonymous letter that detailed some of the accounting manipulations.

When Lay did not respond to her letter at the all-employee meeting, Watkins admitted her authorship to the vice-president of human resources, and set up a meeting with Lay to discuss it. Prior to the meeting, she further documented the fraud and shared the information with a trusted colleague, an in-house lawyer who, unknown to Watkins, had profited from a Fastow SPE. The Enron lawyer accused Watkins of attempting to destroy the company and directed her to meet with Enron's chief legal counsel, who counseled Watkins to maintain silence and cancel her meeting with Lay.

Watkins, unsure what to do, contacted a different social group member, a former accounting colleague who still worked for Arthur Andersen. He encouraged Watkins to abide by the highest accounting standards and professional obligations. This meant disregarding the recommendation from Enron's legal department and informing Lay about the accounting scandal. Meanwhile, another trusted colleague employed at Enron, who had been reassigned to a new position after losing an internal political battle with Fastow, suggested she drop the matter.

Motivated by the highest ethical standard—exposing the truth to someone who could do something about it—she overcame her own personal concerns about being fired and pressure from colleagues to maintain silence. As she had been warned, Lay immediately took Fastow's side on the issue and dismissed Watkins's well-documented concerns. Fastow attempted to fire Watkins when he found out about her private meeting with Lay. Instead, the human resources department followed the advice of the legal department and transferred her to another area to avoid a whistle-blowing lawsuit.

After battling the corporate culture and internal politics on a daily basis for nearly a month, Watkins gave up. Rather than anonymously informing the SEC, Watkins remained loyal to Lay and kept her silence until contacted by a journalist after Enron declared bankruptcy.

Since 1986, people blowing the whistle on illegal activities by organizations doing business with the federal government have had legal protection against employer retaliation and can receive up to 25 percent of any fraudulent monies recovered. States and the federal government further strengthened whistle-blowing laws after the Enron scandal. The Sarbanes-Oxley Act of 2002, which governs publicly held firms, establishes a prison sentence of up to ten years for executives who retaliate against whistle-blowers. Nonetheless, the 2005 National Business Ethics Survey reported that, of the 52 percent of employee respondents who observed ethical misconduct at work, only 55 percent reported them.[461]

Dealing with Unethical Customers

Enron was a relatively minor client for the corporate Arthur Andersen firm, but it was the Houston office's major client. Enron offered corporate jobs to compliant Andersen auditors, with wages and perks far in excess of what they earned at Andersen. Andersen auditors were sometimes reviewing the accounting work of a former boss or colleague, people whose integrity they trusted.

David Duncan, the lead auditor on Arthur Andersen's Enron engagement team, had previously been a colleague of Rick Causey, a former Andersen accountant who became Enron's chief accounting officer. Duncan's annual bonus and career progress depended on continually increasing client fees by 20 percent. Carl Bass, a member of the engagement team, pressured Duncan to reject some of Enron's more egregious accounting methods.

This is the decision Duncan faced at the end of the section titled "Conquering Checks and Balances: 1996 and 1997." Duncan could either demand that Fastow and Causey follow more rigorous accounting standards prior to signing off on the next audit or allow them to violate accounting standards.

Applying the Six Ethical Questions. (1) The primary stakeholders in this particular situation include Duncan, Fastow, Causey, Enron, Arthur Andersen, and investors. (2) Considering only his own interests, Duncan risks losing the Enron account if he demands that Fastow and Causey adopt more rigorous accounting standards. It would negatively impact his bonus and potentially ruin his career at Arthur Andersen. However, if detected, he could be fired and lose his accounting license. (3) There are similar conflicting answers when social group analysis is performed. Duncan's accounting colleagues recommended that he apply more rigorous standards. However, there were several other lead auditors at Andersen who were approving aggressive accounting techniques in order to increase customer satisfaction. (4) Enron's accounting practices were in violation of Generally Accepted Accounting Principles, and auditors have a legal obligation to truthfully validate financial statements.

(5) Signing off on financial statements that violate accounting standards misleads those who rely on them to make informed decisions. Andersen's Houston office was dependent on the $50 million in fees they earned on the Enron account. But Arthur Andersen's already tarnished reputation could be further damaged if the SEC found out about the financial misrepresentation. (6) In addition, the financial statements would not honestly convey information to shareholders, whose interests auditors represent.

Based on these answers to the six ethical framework questions, Duncan should enforce higher accounting standards for the Enron account because that is his professional duty and also his responsibility to investors. The creative challenge is to determine how to do this in a way that does not result in losing Enron as a valued client. Causey's accounting decisions are being unduly influenced by Fastow. Causey needs to be separated from Fastow and reminded of his professional obligations, both to the accounting profession and to stockholders.

Duncan, as Causey's friend, might be able to influence Causey directly. But Duncan was much younger than Causey, and mentors are not necessarily receptive to receiving advice from their protégés. If this is the case, Duncan should inform the board of directors' audit committee chairperson and together develop a strategy to make the necessary changes. A board member must step in and shift Causey's allegiance away from Fastow and toward GAAP.

Carl Bass continued to question Enron's accounting methods. But pressure from Enron and within Andersen led him to accept a different assignment. With Bass out of the way, Fastow and Causey continued to illegally account for SPE transactions. Then Bass joined Arthur Andersen's PSG, which gave him even greater authority to rule on contentious accounting issues. Bass, with the power authorized by his new position, instructed Duncan to inform Enron's board of directors about the company's risky accounting techniques, a request Duncan ignored. Causey and other Enron executives requested that Bass be prevented from commenting on Enron transactions from his new position. To its later regret, Andersen agreed to this request and removed the Enron account from Bass's oversight portfolio.

Outside lawyers and investment bankers faced similar ethical dilemmas. Enron was Vinson & Elkins's largest client. Likewise, board members were beholden to Enron through very generous stock options, and investment bankers through their SPE investments. Raising legitimate objections could damage Enron's financial standing with Wall Street, resulting in a massive stock sell-off and downward spiral, a momentum the board, investment bankers, and external lawyers wanted to avoid for personal reasons.

Fastow continually guaranteed investment bankers a very profitable return-on-investment for their participation in prepay schemes and SPEs. Rejecting Fastow's offers would probably result in losing annual performance bonuses, profits from the transactions, and future fees from Enron. Accepting the illegal offers could possibly result in losing their professional license and damaging their company's reputation. Several investment bankers complained to Enron about Fastow's strong-arm tactics. But, reinforced by the sense that other investment bankers were participating in the schemes, Enron's top-tier investment bankers usually accepted Fastow's offers and then hid this information from Arthur Andersen auditors.

Engaging in deals with unethical customers will stain an organization's reputation and could lead to its downfall. Merrill Lynch, J. P. Morgan Chase, Citigroup, and Credit Suisse First Boston settled multibillion lawsuits with investors as a result of their Enron and WorldCom transactions. Arthur Andersen lost almost all of its customers when it was indicted for obstruction of justice in shredding Enron-related documents. The firm disintegrated when found guilty by a jury, despite the ruling having been overturned by the United States Supreme Court on appeal.

Informing the Public about Financial Problems

In mid-August 2001, Skilling resigned and Lay resumed Enron's CEO duties. He met with executives to assess company operations, and realized that Fastow and Causey had hidden losses totaling $7 billion the past few years without his knowledge. Officially, Enron had $12.8 billion of debt, but the actual amount was approximately $35 billion. Several Enron executives recommended that the company report only $1.2 billion of the $7 billion in losses for the third quarter because that amount could be reasonably explained without significant damage to Enron's already falling stock price. If Lay reported all $7 billion in losses on October 16, there would be a massive stock sell-off, which would lead to a government investigation. A stock price plunge could cause Enron to default on its loans and quickly bankrupt the company.

This is the decision Lay faced at the end of the section titled "Preparing to Announce Third-Quarter Results: September and October 2001." Should Lay announce $7 billion in losses and risk financial collapse, $2 billion in losses to match Wall Street expectations, or $1.2 billion as recommended by some executives?

Applying the Six Ethical Questions. (1) The primary

stakeholders in this particular situation include Lay, Enron, investors, and lenders. (2) Announcing any loss would have a negative effect on Lay, though announcing a $7 billion loss would be the most damaging. Lay could minimize the impact by shifting the blame to the now-departed Skilling, who deserved it. Nonetheless, the losses were attributed to activities that occurred during his previous tenure as CEO, and he must bear the responsibility for inadequate oversight. (3 and 4) Corporate executives have a legal obligation to honestly convey financial information to stockholders. (5 and 6) This is the law because sharing the truth with the public would permit millions of Enron shareholders and its many lenders to make well-informed investment decisions. Some of Enron's 20,000 employees may lose their jobs, but the credibility of the stock market is at risk.

Based on these answers to the six ethical framework questions, Lay should share this information with his board of directors and report the entire $7 billion in hidden losses. Stock prices can decline when companies miss earning projections by a penny, so the creative challenge is in managing the public story, finding a way to share this information that doesn't destroy the company. Some Wall Street analysts had already created the expectation that Enron would report losses as high as $2 billion. These analysts should be immediately contacted and provided a more accurate picture, so that when the actual numbers get released, they fall within the revised expectations.

Enron's stock, along with every other energy company stock, had been in decline all year and was selling between $30 and $35 a share the first two weeks of October. A stock bailout could occur, but it might be slightly more gradual. Many of the short-term investors had already bailed out. Enron's stock took its biggest hit after the SEC announced its formal inquiry into company affairs, and as information began to appear in the press outlining years of misconduct. The only hope for Enron at this juncture is a clean slate, including Lay's resignation, and a solid business plan.

Instead, Lay chose what he considered the more conservative option, announcing only $1.2 billion in losses in such a way that even the journalists who covered the company did not fully understand them. This led to increased suspicion at a time when trust should have been developed. As a result, journalists and analysts became doubtful of any information coming out of the company. Within six weeks Enron had declared bankruptcy and Lay faced lawsuits and criminal indictments for lying to the public.

Seven Moral Levees

Organizational growth is natural. Successful long-term growth requires honesty, trust, integrity, and credibility, among other ethical values. Some managers misrepresent ethics as a cost, rather than a revenue generator. There are startup costs to consider because it takes time to build trust. But these costs are an investment in the future. Organizations with a well-fortified ethical culture tend to have higher degrees of employee, customer, supplier, and investor satisfaction and loyalty.[462] These long-term trusting relationships directly benefit the bottom line.

As shown in the diagram, creating and sustaining an ethical culture requires building a series of seven moral levees around an individual's freedom to pursue his or her self-interests in a competitive business environment where wealth and power are highly valued.

Preservation of the Free Market System

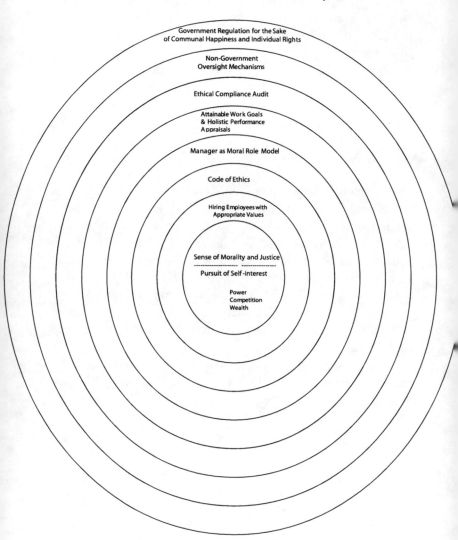

Government Regulation for the Sake
of Communal Happiness and Individual Rights

Non-Government
Oversight Mechanisms

Ethical Compliance Audit

Attainable Work Goals
& Holistic Performance
Appraisals

Manager as Moral Role Model

Code of Ethics

Hiring Employees with
Appropriate Values

Sense of Morality and Justice
--------------------- ---------------
Pursuit of Self-Interest

Power
Competition
Wealth

Moral Levee #1: Hiring Employees with Appropriate Values

When you hire someone you hire that person's ethics as well as skills and expertise. Employees bring their perceptions of right and wrong with them to work.

Organizations should conduct character checks at all levels of organizational hiring. It is important to understand the value system of the employee being hired. Hiring just one employee with an inappropriate value system—someone whose sense of morality and justice does not match the desired corporate culture—can corrupt an entire organization. If left alone, the employee will attract like-minded people and lead them in directions that are likely to be detrimental to organizational operations.

Integrity tests, the easiest and most often used method to screen potential employees for unethical propensities, are prone to false positives because people who lie on them outscore more honest job applicants. Personal interviews are a more reliable method for gauging a person's ethics. Job finalists can be asked to tell stories about the ethics of his or her previous boss or work culture. They can also respond to several complex ethical dilemmas developed by current employees highlighting real-life scenarios that occurred in the past.

Moral Levee #2: Code of Ethics

An organization's code of ethics should be a living document. Provisions within the code of ethics must be consistently enforced to make them meaningful.

Employees should evaluate how well the company is "walking the talk" on an annual basis as a part of employee training and development workshops. Each code statement (that is, "We exhibit high respect for our customers") could be measured on a five-point Likert scale. Training participants should then provide stories about situations that demonstrate high compliance and less than high compliance. Employee feedback should not impact performance evaluations; otherwise, only socially desirable responses will be offered.

Moral Levee #3: The Manager as Moral Role Model

Managers who want employees to exhibit ethical behaviors must themselves behave ethically. Employees receive cues for appropriate behaviors directly from their managers. If a manager sacrifices ethics to accomplish a short-term goal, then employees seeking approval from that manager will probably do likewise. Loyalty matters a great deal in most organizations. Employees seeking managerial approval tend to replicate their direct manager's attitudes and behavior patterns.

Managers must encourage and listen to employees who report unethical activities at the workplace, and respond appropriately. Many employees are hesitant to exercise the required moral courage because they fear retaliation or do not want to be labeled "moral prudes" or "squealers" and ostracized by coworkers.

Moral Levee #4: Attainable Work Goals and Holistic Performance Appraisals

Employees also receive moral expectation cues from work goals and performance appraisals. Some employees will find unethical ways to achieve unattainable work goals in order to protect their jobs or receive a bonus or promotion. Performance appraisals should be directly linked to employee goals. Organizational ethics are enhanced when employees making ethical decisions are financially rewarded and promoted and those making unethical ones are dismissed.

Managers can hold all employees accountable to high ethical standards through holistic performance appraisals. Behaviors and attitudes that impact organizational ethics should be quantified as part of an employee's performance review. A phrase such as "s/he is trustworthy" is subject to a wide interpretation. "S/he promptly handles customer complaints" is a more objective measure of trustworthiness.

Moral Levee #5: Ethical Compliance Audit

Ethical risks must be identified and managed. Managers should seek to create a defect-free ethical culture, one that rejects unethical behaviors, by applying total quality management analysis to ethical deviancies. Employees should track unethical behaviors to their systemic cause, develop appropriate corrective metrics and benchmarks, and then be held accountable for accomplishing the desired results.

This activity should be part of an annual comprehensive, organization-wide ethical compliance audit. Managers can gather information regarding company relations with owners, employees, customers, suppliers, the community, and the natural environment and share it with employees. Appropriate remedies should be implemented to reduce gaps between the ethical ideal and actual performance.

Moral Levee #6: External Non-Government Oversight Mechanisms

The first five moral levees are all internal to the organization. The sixth moral levee is external to the organization and more directly related to preserving the free market system. The organization's ethical analysis and performance needs to be reviewed by an outside source that is not directly involved in company operations. These outside sources have different reference points and can provide valuable feedback, either verifying or contradicting the organization's self-assessment.

Auditors, lawyers, and outside boards of directors represent the standards of external constituencies. They should be treated as independent agents rather than employees of the organization. Auditors are essential for verifying that the organization's financial statements are in compliance with accounting standards. Similarly, lawyers have a professional obligation to uphold legal standards, and outside board members must represent the interests of stockholders and other constituencies. Converting auditors, lawyers, and outside board members to the company's point of view is achieved to the detriment of the organization, as illustrated in the case of Enron.

Moral Levee #7: Government Regulation

Establishing government regulation as the seventh moral levee may seem contradictory. But regulators serve a police function. Although most people are very good, not everyone is. The presence of a police officer enhances the freedom of law-abiding people by restraining the actions of those tempted to engage in unethical activities. Government regulators remove participants from the playing field when they violate the rules of fair competition, which helps to preserve the free market system.

In addition, government regulations clarify minimum moral expectations that can help shape an organization's code of ethics. Regulations inform managers that they cannot sexually harass employees, discriminate against employees for racial or religious reasons, or pollute the environment beyond an agreed-upon amount. These prohibitions should be internalized in codes of ethics that, if followed, reduce burdensome government oversight.

The seven moral levees enhance ethical behaviors, protect organizations from unethical behaviors, and help to ensure the preservation of the free market system. The pursuit of self-interest in a highly competitive environment, which offers huge financial rewards to those who obtain the most power, must take place within a system of checks and balances supportive of ethical organizational cultures. A moral levee with a small leak must be repaired and supported by other moral levees. Otherwise, the levee could be breached, the entire organization could be destroyed, and we end up with harsh patches such as Sarbanes-Oxley. Good things happen and unique opportunities open up when individuals and organizations operate with a clear conscience.

ACKNOWLEDGMENTS

Madison, Wisconsin is often ranked near the top of the most livable cities in the United States. Edgewood College, situated on picturesque Lake Wingra, is an oasis within the city. Many administrators, faculty, and staff embody the school's five Dominican values—Truth, Justice, Partnership, Compassion, and Community—and I'm glad that they do. Being idealistic is both natural and expected at Edgewood College, making it an ideal working and studying environment.

In particular, I wish to thank the full-time faculty and staff of the Business Department, as well as certain Edgewood College alumni, who have greatly enriched my understanding and experience of business: Gary Schroeder, Moses Altsech, Diane Ballweg, Mark Barnard, Elaine Beaubien, Jill Beinborn, Phil Brereton, Mike Cavill, Neil Fauerbach, Dan Gerland, Lisa Goldthorpe, Patricia Hallinan, Fazel Hayati, Ken Macur, Dick Pilsner, Bruce Roberts, Melissa Seeberger, Ken Spuda, and Al Talarczyk. I'm glad I've found a home here.

Lastly, I thank Karen Kodner and Dianne Jenkins for their expert editing skills, Neil Salkind for his publishing advice, and Bill Frederick for his kindness and constructive feedback.

REFERENCES

1 Robert Bryce, *Pipe Dreams: Greed, Ego, and the Death of Enron* (New York: Public Affairs, 2002), 23.

2 Bryce, *Pipe Dreams* 25.

3 Bryce, *Pipe Dreams,* 26.

4 Information on Lay's biography taken from: Bryce, *Pipe Dreams,* 26–30; Kurt Eichenwald, *Conspiracy of Fools* (New York: Broadway Books, 2005), pp. 20–24; Mary Flood, "The Fall of Enron," *Houston Chronicle,* July 9, 2004, A15; Laura Goldberg and Mary Flood, "The Fall of Enron," *Houston Chronicle,* February 3, 2002, A1; James V. Grimaldi, "Endowed By Enron," *Washington Post,* May 12, 2002, F1; Bethany McLean and Peter Elkind, *The Smartest Guys in the Room* (New York: Portfolio, 2003, 2–11; Peter Shinkle, "Head of Besieged Enron Steps Down," *St. Louis Post-Dispatch,* January 24, 2002, A1; Mimi Swartz and Sherron Watkins, *Power Failure* (New York: Currency Doubleday, 2003), 21–27; Evan Thomas and Andrew Murr, "The Gambler Who Blew It All," *Newsweek*, February 4, 2002, 18ff.

5 McLean and Elkind, *The Smartest Guys in the Room,* 7.

6 Bryce, *Pipe Dreams,* 32.

7 Bryce, *Pipe Dreams,* 33.

8 Swartz and Watkins, *Power Failure,* 29.

9 Swartz and Watkins, *Power Failure,* 29.

[10] Eichenwald, *Conspiracy of Fools,* 30-31.

[11] Bryce, *Pipe Dreams,* 31.

[12] McLean and Elkind, *The Smartest Guys in the Room,* 14.

[13] Bryce, *Pipe Dreams,* 37-43; Eichenwald, *Conspiracy of Fools,* 15-20; Swartz and Watkins, *Power Failure,* 31-2.

[14] For Skilling's biography see: Bryce, *Pipe Dreams,* pp. 48-51; Eichenwald, *Conspiracy of Fools,* 26-29; McLean and Elkind, *The Smartest Guys in the Room,* 27-33; Swartz and Watkins, *Power Failure,* 40-44.

[15] McLean and Elkind, *The Smartest Guys in the Room,* 30.

[16] Thomas C. Hayes, "Bottom-Fishing in the Gas Patch," *New York Times,* May 19, 1991, sec. 3, 1 and 6.

[17] Hayes, "Bottom-Fishing," 1.

[18] Eichenwald, *Conspiracy of Fools,* 43-44.

[19] Hayes, "Bottom-Fishing," 1.

[20] Bryce, *Pipe Dreams,* 64.

[21] Swartz and Watkins, *Power Failure,* 23.

[22] Bryce, *Pipe Dreams,* 87-88.

[23] Bryce, *Pipe Dreams,* 54.

[24] Hayes, "Bottom-Fishing," 1.

[25] Bryce, *Pipe Dreams,* 53-56.

[26] Hayes, "Bottom-Fishing," 1.

[27] McLean and Elkind, *The Smartest Guys in the Room,* 87.

[28] Brian Cruver, *Anatomy of Greed* (New York: Carroll & Graf Publishers, 2002), 5.

[29] Cruver, *Anatomy of Greed,* 17-18.

[30] Bryce, *Pipe Dreams,* 201-204; Eichenwald, *Conspiracy of Fools,* 51; McLean and Elkind, *The Smartest Guys in the Room,* 134-137; Swartz and Watkins, *Power Failure,* 152-156.

31 Eichenwald, *Conspiracy of Fools,* 50.

32 Swartz and Watkins, *Power Failure,* 73.

33 Andrew Osterland, "New Rules for Special-Purpose Entities May Result in Bigger Corporate Balance Sheets," *CFO Magazine,* May 2002; Anonymous, "Accounting for Special Purpose Entities Revised: FASB Interpretation 46 (R)," *The CPA Journal* 74, no. 7 (July 2004): , 30.

34 Arthur L. Berkowitz, *Enron: A Professional's Guide to the Events, Ethical Issues, and Proposed Reforms* (Chicago: CCH Incorporated, 2002), 5.

35 Osterland, "New Rules"; Anonymous, "Accounting for Special Purpose Entities," 30.

36 Hayes, "Bottom-Fishing," 1.

37 Eichenwald, *Conspiracy of Fools,* 55.

38 Rebecca Smith and John R. Emshwiller, *24 Days* (New York: Harper Books, 2003), 78.

39 Bryce, *Pipe Dreams,* 67-68.

40 Bryce, *Pipe Dreams,* 72-73; McLean and Elkind, *The Smartest Guys in the Room,* 48-49.

41 McLean and Elkind, *The Smartest Guys in the Room,* 45-46.

42 Bryce, *Pipe Dreams,* 74.

43 McLean and Elkind, *The Smartest Guys in the Room,* 46.

44 McLean and Elkind, *The Smartest Guys in the Room,* 48.

45 Cruver, *Anatomy of Greed,* 48 and 101.

46 Bryce, *Pipe Dreams,* 81.

47 Bryce, *Pipe Dreams,* 104-106.

48 McLean and Elkind, *The Smartest Guys in the Room,* 93.

49 Bryce, *Pipe Dreams,* 114.

50 McLean and Elkind, *The Smartest Guys in the Room,* 152.

[51] McLean and Elkind, *The Smartest Guys in the Room,* 159.

[52] McLean and Elkind, *The Smartest Guys in the Room,* 150-170.

[53] McLean and Elkind, *The Smartest Guys in the Room,* 142-143.

[54] Swartz and Watkins, *Power Failure,* 64.

[55] Tony Allison, "Enron's Eight-Year Power Struggle in India," *Asia Times Online,* January 18, 2001; Daniel Pearl, "In India, Other Firms Feel Enron's Pain," *Wall Street Journal*, July 5, 2001.

[56] Bryce, *Pipe Dreams,* 93-103.

[57] Swartz and Watkins, *Power Failure,* 68.

[58] McLean and Elkind, *The Smartest Guys in the Room,* 94-95; Swartz & Watkins, pp. 69-70.

[59] McLean and Elkind, *The Smartest Guys in the Room,* 95; Swartz & Watkins, pp. 69-70.

[60] McLean and Elkind, *The Smartest Guys in the Room,* 85.

[61] Swartz and Watkins, *Power Failure,* 136.

[62] McLean and Elkind, *The Smartest Guys in the Room,* 96.

[63] McLean and Elkind, *The Smartest Guys in the Room,* 90.

[64] Bryce, *Pipe Dreams,* 152-154.

[65] Bryce, *Pipe Dreams,* 149-50; Cruver, *Anatomy of Greed,* 73.

[66] Bryce, *Pipe Dreams,* 4; McLean and Elkind, *The Smartest Guys in the Room,* 86.

[67] Smith and Emshwiller, *24 Days,* 7.

[68] Eichenwald, *Conspiracy of Fools,* 78-88.

[69] Bryce, *Pipe Dreams,* 116.

[70] Swartz and Watkins, *Power Failure,* 88-92.

[71] Bryce, *Pipe Dreams,* 117-119; Eichenwald, *Conspiracy of Fools,* 119-120.

72 Michael Davis, "Lay Staying, So Kinder Will Leave," *Houston Chronicle,* November 27, 1996, 1.

73 McLean and Elkind, *The Smartest Guys in the Room,* 98.

74 McLean and Elkind, *The Smartest Guys in the Room,* 100.

75 Eichenwald, *Conspiracy of Fools,* 127; McLean and Elkind, *The Smartest Guys in the Room,* 101.

76 Eichenwald, *Conspiracy of Fools,* 131.

77 Smith and Emshwiller, *24 Days,* 40.

78 McLean and Elkind, *The Smartest Guys in the Room,* 313.

79 McLean and Elkind, *The Smartest Guys in the Room,* 151.

80 Eichenwald, *Conspiracy of Fools,* 104-106.

81 Cruver, *Anatomy of Greed,* 26.

82 McLean and Elkind, *The Smartest Guys in the Room,* 106.

83 "Deregulation Deception: Harvard, Enron, and the Alliance to Deregulate Electricity Markets in California and Beyond," *A Harvard Watch Report,* May 21, 2002.

84 McLean and Elkind, *The Smartest Guys in the Room,* 107; Swartz and Watkins, *Power Failure,* 114.

85 Bryce, *Pipe Dreams,* 113.

86 Bryce, *Pipe Dreams,* 73-74; Cruver, *Anatomy of Greed,* 179; McLean and Elkind, *The Smartest Guys in the Room,* 103-104.

87 Swartz and Watkins, *Power Failure,* 160.

88 *USA v. Lea W. Fastow,* April 30, 2003, 6.

89 McLean and Elkind, *The Smartest Guys in the Room,* 167; Swartz and Watkins, *Power Failure,* 211; *USA v. Lea W. Fastow,* April 30, 2003, 3-4.

90 *USA v. Lea W. Fastow,* April 30, 2003, 3-5.

91 *SEC v. Andrew S. Fastow,* October, 2002, 5.

[92] Bryce, *Pipe Dreams,* 140; Eichenwald, *Conspiracy of Fools,* 155.

[93] Eichenwald, *Conspiracy of Fools,* 164.

[94] Eichenwald, *Conspiracy of Fools,* 162.

[95] Bryce, *Pipe Dreams,* 139-143; Swartz and Watkins, *Power Failure,* 161-163.

[96] Cruver, *Anatomy of Greed,* 61-64.

[97] Cruver, *Anatomy of Greed,* 181.

[98] McLean and Elkind, *The Smartest Guys in the Room,* 154.

[99] Eichenwald, *Conspiracy of Fools,* 55 and 138-139.

[100] McLean and Elkind, *The Smartest Guys in the Room,* 146.

[101] Bryce, *Pipe Dreams,* 113.

[102] Eichenwald, *Conspiracy of Fools,* 140.

[103] Eichenwald, *Conspiracy of Fools,* 149-150.

[104] Berkowitz, *Enron: A Professional's Guide,* 3.

[105] Eichenwald, *Conspiracy of Fools,* 165.

[106] McLean and Elkind, *The Smartest Guys in the Room,* 105.

[107] Bryce, *Pipe Dreams,* 133.

[108] Bryce, *Pipe Dreams,* 134; Swartz and Watkins, *Power Failure,* 191-192.

[109] Bryce, *Pipe Dreams,* 264.

[110] Swartz and Watkins, *Power Failure,* 227.

[111] McLean and Elkind, *The Smartest Guys in the Room,* 105.

[112] Cruver, *Anatomy of Greed,* 273.

[113] Eichenwald, *Conspiracy of Fools,* 172.

[114] McLean and Elkind, *The Smartest Guys in the Room,* 125.

[115] Cruver, *Anatomy of Greed,* 81.

[116] Eichenwald, *Conspiracy of Fools,* 173-175.

[117] Eichenwald, *Conspiracy of Fools,* 184.

[118] McLean and Elkind, *The Smartest Guys in the Room,* 113 and 249.

[119] McLean and Elkind, *The Smartest Guys in the Room,* 247.

[120] Eichenwald, *Conspiracy of Fools,* 190.

[121] Bryce, *Pipe Dreams,* 67-68.

[122] Swartz and Watkins, *Power Failure,* 127.

[123] Eichenwald, *Conspiracy of Fools,* 186.

[124] McLean and Elkind, *The Smartest Guys in the Room,* 249.

[125] Eichenwald, *Conspiracy of Fools,* 191; Smith and Emshwiller, *24 Days,* 138.

[126] Tom Fowler, "The Enron Tangle," *Houston Chronicle*, November 8, 2001, 1.

[127] Berkowitz, *Enron: A Professional Guide,* 3.

[128] McLean and Elkind, *The Smartest Guys in the Room,* 321.

[129] Bryce, *Pipe Dreams,* 113.

[130] Eichenwald, *Conspiracy of Fools,* 355; *USA v. Lea W. Fastow,* April 30, 2003, p. 6.

[131] Swartz and Watkins, *Power Failure,* 145.

[132] McLean and Elkind, *The Smartest Guys in the Room,* 163.

[133] McLean and Elkind, *The Smartest Guys in the Room,* 155-156.

[134] Bryce, *Pipe Dreams,* 156.

[135] Swartz and Watkins, *Power Failure,* 127.

[136] John Cassidy, *dot.com* (New York: HarperCollins, 2002), 196.

[137] McLean and Elkind, *The Smartest Guys in the Room,* 253.

[138] Eichenwald, *Conspiracy of Fools,* 240.

[139] Cassidy, *dot.com,* 200.

[140] Bryce, *Pipe Dreams,* 288.

[141] McLean and Elkind, *The Smartest Guys in the Room,* 191.

[142] McLean and Elkind, *The Smartest Guys in the Room,* 191.

[143] Bryce, *Pipe Dreams,* 155-159; McLean and Elkind, *The Smartest Guys in the Room,* 191-197; Swartz and Watkins, *Power Failure,* 166-168.

[144] Bryce, *Pipe Dreams,* 157-159; McLean and Elkind, *The Smartest Guys in the Room,* 193.

[145] McLean and Elkind, *The Smartest Guys in the Room,* 192.

[146] McLean and Elkind, *The Smartest Guys in the Room,* 193.

[147] Eichenwald, *Conspiracy of Fools,* 252-255.

[148] Eichenwald, *Conspiracy of Fools,* 331.

[149] Eichenwald, *Conspiracy of Fools,* 238.

[150] Eichenwald, *Conspiracy of Fools,* 247.

[151] Eichenwald, *Conspiracy of Fools,* 250.

[152] Eichenwald, *Conspiracy of Fools,* 261.

[153] Eichenwald, *Conspiracy of Fools,* 260.

[154] Allison, "Enron's Eight-Year Power Struggle," 9.

[155] Bryce, *Pipe Dreams,* 173.

[156] Bryce, *Pipe Dreams,* 157-158.

[157] *USA v. Causey, Skilling, and Lay,* July 7, 2004, 15.

[158] Eichenwald, *Conspiracy of Fools,* 251.

[159] Eichenwald, *Conspiracy of Fools,* 440.

[160] McLean and Elkind, *The Smartest Guys in the Room,* 198-201.

161 Smith and Emshwiller, *24 Days*, 51.

162 McLean and Elkind, *The Smartest Guys in the Room*, 164.

163 McLean and Elkind, *The Smartest Guys in the Room*, 202.

164 Eichenwald, *Conspiracy of Fools*, p. 268.

165 Bryce, *Pipe Dreams*, 163.

166 Eichenwald, *Conspiracy of Fools*, 263.

167 McLean and Elkind, *The Smartest Guys in the Room*, 210.

168 Eichenwald, *Conspiracy of Fools*, 289-290.

169 McLean and Elkind, *The Smartest Guys in the Room*, 253-258.

170 McLean and Elkind, *The Smartest Guys in the Room*, 221-223.

171 Bryce, *Pipe Dreams*, 217.

172 Bryce, *Pipe Dreams*, 225.

173 McLean and Elkind, *The Smartest Guys in the Room*, 204.

174 Bryce, *Pipe Dreams*, 225.

175 *USA v. Bayly, Brown and Furst*, September 16, 2003, 3-10; McLean and Elkind, *The Smartest Guys in the Room*, 208-209; Swartz and Watkins, *Power Failure*, 216-218.

176 *USA v. Bayly, Boyle, Brown, Fuhs, Furst, and Kahanek*, October 14, 2003, 2.

177 Bryce, *Pipe Dreams*, 113.

178 McLean and Elkind, *The Smartest Guys in the Room*, 242.

179 Eichenwald, *Conspiracy of Fools*, 301.

180 McLean and Elkind, *The Smartest Guys in the Room*, 240-241.

181 *USA v. Lea W. Fastow*, April 30, 2003, 11.

182 Eichenwald, *Conspiracy of Fools*, 283.

183 Cassidy, *dot.com*, 261.

[184] Om Malik, *Broadbandits: Inside the $750 Billion Telecom Heist* (Hoboken, N.J.: John Wiley & Sons, 2003), 102.

[185] Swartz and Watkins, *Power Failure,* 179.

[186] Malik, *Broadbandits,* 102; McLean and Elkind, *The Smartest Guys in the Room,* 243.

[187] *USA v. Causey, Skilling, and Lay,* July 7, 2004, 21-22.

[188] *USA v. Causey, Skilling, and Lay,* July 7, 2004, 21-22.

[189] Eichenwald, *Conspiracy of Fools,* 307.

[190] *USA v. Causey, Skilling, and Lay,* July 7, 2004, 61.

[191] McLean and Elkind, *The Smartest Guys in the Room,* 187.

[192] Eichenwald, *Conspiracy of Fools,* 318 and 328.

[193] Eichenwald, *Conspiracy of Fools,* 291.

[194] Smith and Emschwiller, *24 Days,* 54.

[195] McClean and Elkind, *The Smartest Guys in the Room,* 154.

[196] Eichenwald, *Conspiracy of Fools,* 348.

[197] *USA v. Michael J. Kopper,* August 20, 2002, 10.

[198] Bryce, *Pipe Dreams,* 227.

[199] Swartz and Watkins, *Power Failure,* 214.

[200] For explanations of this see: Bryce, *Pipe Dreams,* 227-228; McLean and Elkind, *The Smartest Guys in the Room,* 194-197; Swartz and Watkins, *Power Failure,* 212-214; *USA v. Andrew S. Fastow,* October 31, 2002, 14; *USA v. Michael J. Kopper,* August 20, 2002, 11.

[201] Also referred to as Talon.

[202] Smith and Emshwiller, *24 Days,* 51.

[203] Eichenwald, *Conspiracy of Fools,* 406.

[204] Eichenwald, *Conspiracy of Fools,* 375–376; Smith and Emsh-

willer, *24 Days*, 289.

205 Eichenwald, *Conspiracy of Fools*, 327.

206 Swartz and Watkins, *Power Failure*, 203.

207 Bryce, *Pipe Dreams*, 216.

208 Bryce, *Pipe Dreams*, 280; McLean and Elkind, *The Smartest Guys in the Room*, 289–290.

209 Eichenwald, *Conspiracy of Fools*, 354.

210 *USA v. Causey, Skilling, and Lay*, July 7, 2004, 23.

211 McLean and Elkind, *The Smartest Guys in the Room*, 309.

212 *USA v. Causey, Skilling, and Lay*, July 7, 2004, 17.

213 Bryce, *Pipe Dreams*, 230; McLean and Elkind, *The Smartest Guys in the Room*, 290.

214 Bryce, *Pipe Dreams*, 221.

215 McLean and Elkind, *The Smartest Guys in the Room*, 268–269; Swartz and Watkins, *Power Failure*, 240.

216 Eichenwald, *Conspiracy of Fools*, 342–343; McLean and Elkind, *The Smartest Guys in the Room*, 274.

217 Eichenwald, *Conspiracy of Fools*, 358–359.

218 McLean and Elkind, *The Smartest Guys in the Room*, 219.

219 *USA v. Causey, Skilling, and Lay*, July 7, 2004, 24.

220 McLean and Elkind, *The Smartest Guys in the Room*, 291–293.

221 Eichenwald, *Conspiracy of Fools*, 276.

222 Bryce, *Pipe Dreams*, 189.

223 *USA v. Causey, Skilling, and Lay*, July 7, 2004, 59-61.

224 McLean and Elkind, *The Smartest Guys in the Room*, 297; Smith and Emshwiller, *24 Days*, 265.

225 Cassidy, *dot.com*, 304.

[226] Bryce, *Pipe Dreams,* 282.

[227] McLean and Elkind, *The Smartest Guys in the Room,* 297; Smith and Emshwiller, *24 Days,* 265.

[228] Swartz and Watkins, *Power Failure,* 204.

[229] Smith and Emshwiller, *24 Days,* 347.

[230] Allison, "Enron's Eight-Year Power Struggle," 2.

[231] McLean and Elkind, *The Smartest Guys in the Room,* 83.

[232] Swartz and Watkins, *Power Failure,* 205.

[233] Bryce, *Pipe Dreams,* 286.

[234] Eichenwald, *Conspiracy of Fools,* 362.

[235] Bryce, *Pipe Dreams,* 289; Eichenwald, *Conspiracy of Fools,* 372-373.

[236] Bryce, *Pipe Dreams,* 213; McLean and Elkind, *The Smartest Guys in the Room,* 302 and 309.

[237] *USA v. Causey, Skilling, and Lay,* July 7, 2004, 18.

[238] Bryce, *Pipe Dreams,* 289-290.

[239] Malik, *Broadbandits,* 109.

[240] Bryce, *Pipe Dreams,* 280-281.

[241] Malik, *Broadbandits,* 82.

[242] Swartz and Watkins, *Power Failure,* 296.

[243] Smith and Emshwiller, *24 Days,* 278.

[244] Bryce, *Pipe Dreams,* 231.

[245] *USA v. Arthur Andersen,* March 14, 2002, 4-5.

[246] McLean and Elkind, *The Smartest Guys in the Room,* 317; Swartz and Watkins, *Power Failure,* 269-270.

[247] Eichenwald, *Conspiracy of Fools,* 420; McLean and Elkind, *The Smartest Guys in the Room,* 313.

[248] Bryce, *Pipe Dreams,* 211-212; David Denby, *American Sucker* (New York: Little, Brown and Company, 2004), 275.

[249] Cruver, *Anatomy of Greed,* 140.

[250] Bryce, *Pipe Dreams,* 278.

[251] "Deregulation Deception: Harvard, Enron, and the Alliance to Deregulate Electricity Markets in California and Beyond," A *Harvard Watch Report,* May 21, 2002.

[252] Swartz and Watkins, *Power Failure,* 225.

[253] Richard A. Oppel, Jr. and Floyd Norris, "Enron Chief Will Give Up Severance," *New York Times,* November 14, 2001, C1.

[254] *USA v. Causey, Skilling, and Lay,* 2004, 59.

[255] Eichenwald, *Conspiracy of Fools,* 420; *USA v. Lea W. Fastow,* April 30, 2003, 12.

[256] Cruver, *Anatomy of Greed,* 140.

[257] Floyd Norris, "Does Enron Trust Its New Numbers?" *New York Times,* November 9, 2001, C1.

[258] Bethany McLean, "Is Enron Overpriced?" *Fortune,* March 5, 2001, 122.

[259] Bryce, *Pipe Dreams,* 241-243.

[260] Cruver, *Anatomy of Greed,* 25.

[261] Cassidy, *dot.com,* 336.

[262] Swartz and Watkins, *Power Failure,* 206.

[263] McLean and Elkind, *The Smartest Guys in the Room,* 314; *USA v. Causey, Skilling, and Lay,* July 7, 2004, 28.

[264] Michael Davis, "Enron Deal with Sierra Likely a Bust," *Houston Chronicle*, March 24, 2001.

[265] Eichenwald, *Conspiracy of Fools,* 457.

[266] Eichenwald, *Conspiracy of Fools,* 414.

[267] Bryce, *Pipe Dreams*, 270-271.

[268] Bryce, *Pipe Dreams*, 300-304.

[269] Cruver, *Anatomy of Greed*, 271-272.

[270] Allan Turner, "Enron's Fall Shakes Up Nonprofit Community," *Houston Chronicle*, December 7, 2001, A1.

[271] McLean and Elkind, *The Smartest Guys in the Room*, 343-344.

[272] Bryce, *Pipe Dreams*, 317

[273] McLean and Elkind, *The Smartest Guys in the Room*, 353.

[274] Bryce, *Pipe Dreams*, 250.

[275] Cassell Bryan-Low and Suzanne McGee, "What Enron's Financial Reports Did—and Didn't—Reveal," *Wall Street Journal*, November 5, 2001, C1.

[276] McLean and Elkind, *The Smartest Guys in the Room*, 323.

[277] Bryce, *Pipe Dreams*, 210.

[278] Bryce, *Pipe Dreams*, 290.

[279] Bryce, *Pipe Dreams*, 254.

[280] Swartz and Watkins, *Power Failure*, 265.

[281] *USA v. Causey, Skilling, and Lay*, July 7, 2004, 27.

[282] McLean and Elkind, *The Smartest Guys in the Room*, \388.

[283] Simon Romero, "Bandwidth Traders' Uncertain Future," *New York Times*, December 2, 2001, 11.

[284] Smith and Emshwiller, *24 Days*, 265.

[285] Craig Brown, "Blockbuster, Enron Pull the Plug on Plan to Offer Video-on-Demand," *The Oregonian*, April 2, 2001; Tom Fowler, "Blockbuster Joins Enron in Halting Web agreement," *Houston Chronicle*, March 10, 2001; McLean and Elkind, *The Smartest Guys in the Room*, 293-294; Swartz and Watkins, *Power Failure*, 261.

[286] Tom Flower, "Enron Broadband Pares 250 from Its Workforce," *Houston Chronicle*, April 6, 2001.

[287] Don Mills, "Deal Keeps Enron in the Game of Streaming Content on Demand," *National Post*, March 20, 2001.

[288] Bryce, *Pipe Dreams*, 275.

[289] Michael Davis, "Enron Deal with Sierra Likely a Bust," *Houston Chronicle*, March 24, 2001.

[290] Laura Goldberg, "Enron Talks Utility Sale in Oregon," *Houston Chronicle*, October 6, 2001.

[291] McLean and Elkind, *The Smartest Guys in the Room*, 279.

[292] Eichenwald, *Conspiracy of Fools*, 436.

[293] Eichenwald, *Conspiracy of Fools*, 426-428; McLean and Elkind, *The Smartest Guys in the Room*, 317.

[294] Eichenwald, *Conspiracy of Fools*, 421.

[295] Eichenwald, *Conspiracy of Fools*, 437.

[296] *USA v. Causey, Skilling, and Lay*, July 7, 2004.

[297] Bryce, *Pipe Dreams*, 243-244.

[298] Bryce, *Pipe Dreams*, 286.

[299] Cruver, *Anatomy of Greed*, 53.

[300] Bryce, *Pipe Dreams*, 269.

[301] Smith and Emshwiller, *24 Days*, 32.

[302] Bob Sechler, "Enron Strives to Make a Market in Trading Memory-Chip Futures," *Wall Street Journal*, June 8, 2001.

[303] Ralph Bivins, "Firm in a Hurry to Get into New Downtown Tower," *Houston Chronicle*, April 15, 2001.

[304] Bryce, *Pipe Dreams*, 305-308.

[305] Bryce, *Pipe Dreams*, 265.

[306] Cruver, *Anatomy of Greed,* 15.

[307] Eichenwald, *Conspiracy of Fools,* 448; McLean and Elkind, *The Smartest Guys in the Room,* 337.

[308] Michael Davis, "Enron to Sell Assets in Oil, Gas off India," *Houston Chronicle,* October 4, 2001.

[309] McLean and Elkind, *The Smartest Guys in the Room,* 335.

[310] McLean and Elkind, *The Smartest Guys in the Room,* 335.

[311] McLean and Elkind, *The Smartest Guys in the Room,* 343-344.

[312] Bryce, *Pipe Dreams,* 289.

[313] McLean and Elkind, *The Smartest Guys in the Room,* 279.

[314] Eichenwald, *Conspiracy of Fools,* 464.

[315] McLean and Elkind, *The Smartest Guys in the Room,* 336.

[316] McLean and Elkind, *The Smartest Guys in the Room,* 328.

[317] Eichenwald, *Conspiracy of Fools,* 452.

[318] McLean and Elkind, *The Smartest Guys in the Room,* 329.

[319] Bryce, *Pipe Dreams,* 318.

[320] Eichenwald, *Conspiracy of Fools,* 514; McLean and Elkind, *The Smartest Guys in the Room,* 330; Swartz and Watkins, *Power Failure,* 280.

[321] *USA v. Causey, Skilling, and Lay,* July 7, 2004, 1.

[322] Eichenwald, *Conspiracy of Fools,* 471.

[323] Bryce, *Pipe Dreams,* 290-291.

[324] McLean and Elkind, *The Smartest Guys in the Room,* 339.

[325] Rebecca Smith, "Enron's Net Soars, Despite Telecom Loss, Gaining 40% Amid Strong Energy Units," *Wall Street Journal,* July 13, 2001.

[326] McLean and Elkind, *The Smartest Guys in the Room,* 339.

327 McLean and Elkind, *The Smartest Guys in the Room,* 342.

328 McLean and Elkind, *The Smartest Guys in the Room,* 124.

329 Eichenwald, *Conspiracy of Fools,* 474.

330 Bryce, *Pipe Dreams,* 283.

331 Eichenwald, *Conspiracy of Fools,* 476.

332 Swartz and Watkins, *Power Failure,* 272.

333 McLean and Elkind, *The Smartest Guys in the Room,* 347.

334 Jonathan Friedland, "Enron's CEO, Skilling, Quits Two Top Posts," *Wall Street Journal*, August 15, 2001.

335 Eichenwald, *Conspiracy of Fools,* 519; McLean and Elkind, *The Smartest Guys in the Room,* 353.

336 Bryce, *Pipe Dreams,* 296-297.

337 Swartz and Watkins, *Power Failure,* 286.

338 Swartz and Watkins, *Power Failure,* 369-370.

339 Swartz and Watkins, *Power Failure,* 370.

340 Swartz and Watkins, *Power Failure,* 276-280.

341 Swartz and Watkins, *Power Failure,* 284.

342 Cruver, *Anatomy of Greed,* 92.

343 Smith and Emshwiller, *24 Days,* 19-20.

344 John R. Emshwiller, "Enron's Skilling Cites Stock Price Plunge as Main Reasons for Leaving CEO Post," *Wall Street Journal*, August 16, 2001.

345 Laura Goldberg and Mary Flood, "The Fall of Enron," *Houston Chronicle*, February 3, 2002, A1.

346 McLean and Elkind, *The Smartest Guys in the Room,* 353.

347 McLean and Elkind, *The Smartest Guys in the Room,* 350.

348 Swartz and Watkins, *Power Failure,* 279.

[349] Swartz and Watkins, *Power Failure,* 281-283.

[350] Swartz and Watkins, *Power Failure,* 285.

[351] Swartz and Watkins, *Power Failure,* 285-286.

[352] Swartz and Watkins, *Power Failure,* 287.

[353] Bryce, *Pipe Dreams,* 299.

[354] Swartz and Watkins, *Power Failure,* 289.

[355] Bryce, *Pipe Dreams,* 298; McLean and Elkind, *The Smartest Guys in the Room,* 357.

[356] Swartz and Watkins, *Power Failure,* 293.

[357] Eichenwald, *Conspiracy of Fools,* 505.

[358] Bryce, *Pipe Dreams,* 298.

[359] Swartz and Watkins, *Power Failure,* 291.

[360] Eichenwald, *Conspiracy of Fools,* 481.

[361] *USA v. Causey, Skilling, and Lay,* July 7, 2004, 4.

[362] *USA v. Causey, Skilling, and Lay,* July 7, 2004, p. 4.

[363] Rebecca Smith and John Emshwiller, "Enron Prepares to Become Easier to Read," *Wall Street Journal,* August 28, 2001.

[364] *Arthur Andersen v. USA,* Petition for a Writ of Certiorari, Brief for the United States in Opposition, December 2004, 4.

[365] Smith and Emshwiller, *24 Days,* 47-48.

[366] Eichenwald, *Conspiracy of Fools,* 472.

[367] Laura Goldberg, "Two Top Execs Named to Join Enron's Office of Chairman," *Houston Chronicle,* August 29, 2001.

[368] Swartz and Watkins, *Power Failure,* 294.

[369] McLean and Elkind, *The Smartest Guys in the Room,* 362.

[370] Swartz and Watkins, *Power Failure,* 295.

[371] Eichenwald, *Conspiracy of Fools,* 508.

372 Eichenwald, *Conspiracy of Fools,* 514.

373 *USA v. Causey, Skilling, and Lay,* July 7, 2004, 6.

374 *USA v. Causey, Skilling, and Lay,* July 7, 2004, 32.

375 Laura Goldberg, "Enron Seals Deal to Sell Portland General Utility," *Houston Chronicle,* October 9, 2001.

376 McLean and Elkind, *The Smartest Guys in the Room,* 366.

377 Eichenwald, *Conspiracy of Fools,* 506 and 515.

378 Susan E. Squires, Cynthia J. Smith, Lorna McDougall, and William R. Yeachk, *Inside Arthur Andersen: Shifting Values, Unexpected Consequences* (Upper Saddle River, N.J.: Prentice Hall, 2003), 120-122; Barbara Ley Toffler and Jennifer Reingold, *Final Accounting: Ambition, Greed, and the Fall of Arthur Andersen* (New York: Currency Doubleday, 2003), 146-150.

379 McLean and Elkind, *The Smartest Guys in the Room,* 367-368.

380 *USA v. Causey, Skilling, and Lay,* July 7, 2004, 31.

381 Eichenwald, *Conspiracy of Fools,* 520.

382 Eichenwald, *Conspiracy of Fools,* 524.

383 McLean and Elkind, *The Smartest Guys in the Room,* 381-382.

384 Smith and Emshwiller, *24 Days,* 70.

385 Smith and Emshwiller, *24 Days,* 96.

386 Cruver, *Anatomy of Greed,* 115-118.

387 *USA v. Causey, Skilling, and Lay,* July 7, 2004, 33-34.

388 *USA v. Causey, Skilling, and Lay,* July 7, 2004, 33.

389 Smith and Emshwiller, *24 Days,* 113.

390 Shannon Buggs, "Labor Department Examines Enron Retirement Plan," *Houston Chronicle,* December 6, 2001; David Ivanovich, "Labor Probes 401(k) Lockdown," *Houston Chronicle,* January 24, 2002, 14;. Jo Thomas, "Enron's Collapse: Fading Nest

Eggs," *New York Times*, January 23, 2002, 6.

[391] Smith and Emshwiller, *24 Days,* 172.

[392] Cruver, *Anatomy of Greed,* 125.

[393] Eichenwald, *Conspiracy of Fools,* 534.

[394] Cruver, *Anatomy of Greed,* 130-132.

[395] Smith and Emshwiller, *24 Days,* 122.

[396] Smith and Emshwiller, *24 Days,* 125.

[397] Smith and Emshwiller, *24 Days,* 129.

[398] Smith and Emshwiller, *24 Days,* 130.

[399] Rebecca Smith and John R. Emshwiller, "Enron's CFO's Partnership Had Millions in Profit," *Wall Street Journal,* October 19, 2001.

[400] *USA v. Causey, Skilling, and Lay,* July 7, 2004, 34.

[401] McLean and Elkind, *The Smartest Guys in the Room,* 161.

[402] Floyd Norris, "Enron Tries to Dismiss Financial Doubts," *New York Times*, October 24, 2005.

[403] Smith and Emshwiller, *24 Days,* 147 and 173.

[404] Eichenwald, *Conspiracy of Fools,* 549-551.

[405] Smith and Emshwiller, *24 Days,* 294.

[406] *USA v. Arthur Andersen,* March 14, 2002, 5-6.

[407] Eichenwald, *Conspiracy of Fools,* 554.

[408] Bryce, *Pipe Dreams,* 318.

[409] Smith and Emshwiller, *24 Days,* 52.

[410] Eichenwald, *Conspiracy of Fools,* 555 and 558.

[411] Smith and Emshwiller, *24 Days,* 164.

[412] Smith and Emshwiller, *24 Days,* 158.

[413] Swartz and Watkins, *Power Failure,* 317.

414 Bryce, *Pipe Dreams,* 113.

415 Bryce, *Pipe Dreams,* 255.

416 Laura Goldberg, "Action by Enron Halts Stock's Fall," *Houston Chronicle*, October 26, 2001.

417 "Enron Credit Rating Is Cut, and Its Share Price Suffers," *New York Times*, October 30, 2001; Smith and Emshwiller, *24 Days,* 174.

418 Eichenwald, *Conspiracy of Fools,* 589.

419 John R. Emshwiller and Rebecca Smith, "U.S. Regulators Step Up Probe into Enron Dealings," *Wall Street Journal,* November 1, 2001.

420 Richard A. Oppel, Jr. and Andrew Ross Sorkin, "Enron Looks for Investors, but Finds Them Skittish," *New York Times,* November 7, 2001.

421 Eichenwald, *Conspiracy of Fools,* 571.

422 Laura Goldberg, "Dynegy to Acquire Enron in $8.9 Billion Stock Deal," *Houston Chronicle,* November 10, 2001, A1.

423 Eichenwald, *Conspiracy of Fools,* 181.

424 *Arthur Andersen v. USA,* Petition for a Writ of Certiorari, Not Dated, 2004, 9.

425 Eichenwald, *Conspiracy of Fools,* 597.

426 Bryce, *Pipe Dreams,* 328.

427 Smith and Emshwiller, *24 Days,* 185.

428 Bryce, *Pipe Dreams,* 329.

429 Smith and Emshwiller, *24 Days,* 201; Swartz and Watkins, *Power Failure,* 329-332.

430 McLean and Elkind, *The Smartest Guys in the Room,* 395.

431 McLean and Elkind, *The Smartest Guys in the Room,* 392.

432 Alex Berenson and Andrew Ross Sorkin, "Rival to Buy Enron,

Top Energy Trader, After Financial Fall," *New York Times,* November 10, 2001.

[433] Goldberg, "Dynegy to Acquire Enron."

[434] Goldberg, "Dynegy to Acquire Enron."

[435] McLean and Elkind, *The Smartest Guys in the Room,* 397.

[436] Bryce, *Pipe Dreams,* 329; Eichenwald, *Conspiracy of Fools,* 611.

[437] Ivanovich, "Labor Probes 401(k) Lockdown," 14.

[438] Richard A. Oppel, Jr. and Floyd Norris, "Enron Chief Will Give Up Severance," *New York Times,* November 14, 2001.

[439] Smith and Emshwiller, *24 Days,* 204.

[440] McLean and Elkind, *The Smartest Guys in the Room,* 393.

[441] Smith and Emshwiller, *24 Days,* 205.

[442] Tom Fowler, "Enron Plans Asset Sell-off to Slash Debt," *Houston Chronicle,* November 15, 2001.

[443] Cruver, pp. 168-169.

[444] Richard A. Oppel, Jr. and Floyd Norris, "In New Filing, Enron Reports Debt Squeeze," *New York Times,* November 20, 2001.

[445] Eichenwald, p. 619.

[446] Richard A. Oppel, Jr., "Enron's Growing Financial Crisis Raises Doubts about Merger Deal," *New York Times*, November 21, 2001.

[447] Nelson Antosh, "Deal Still on as Enron Shares Drop 6%, *Houston Chronicle*, November 24, 2001; Smith & Emshwiller, p. 207.

[448] Mary Flood, "Sizable Staff of 245 Lawyers in Merger Limbo," *Houston Chronicle*, November 27, 2001.

[449] Richard A. Oppel, Jr. and Andrew Ross Sorkin, "Trying to Restore Confidence in Enron to Salvage a Merger," *New York Times*, November 28, 2001.

450 Cruver, *Anatomy of Greed,* 185; Richard A. Oppel, Jr. and Andrew Ross Sorkin, "Enron Collapses as Suitor Cancels Plans for Merger," *New York Times,* November 29, 2001.

451 Cruver, *Anatomy of Greed,* 189.

452 Bryce, *Pipe Dreams,* 340; Cruver, *Anatomy of Greed,* 233-237.

453 Richard A. Oppel, Jr. and Andrew Ross Sorkin, "Enron Corp. Files Largest U.S. Claim for Bankruptcy," *New York Times,* December 3, 2001.

454 Bryce, *Pipe Dreams,* 339-340.

455 Cruver, *Anatomy of Greed,* 217.

456 Cruver, *Anatomy of Greed,* 222-223.

457 McLean and Elkind, *The Smartest Guys in the Room,* 343.

458 McLean and Elkind, *The Smartest Guys in the Room,* 313 and 350.

459 McLean and Elkind, *The Smartest Guys in the Room,* 376.

460 For a philosophical explanation of these six questions see Denis Collins and Thomas O'Rourke, *Ethical Dilemmas in Business* (Cincinnati, Ohio: South-Western Publishing Company, 1994); or Denis Collins and Laura Page, "A Socrates/Ted Koppel Paradigm for Integrating the Teaching of Business Ethics in the Curriculum," 221-242 in *Research in Corporate Social Performance and Policy,* special issue on "Teaching Business and Society Courses with Reflective and Active Learning Strategies," ed. Sandra Waddock, vol. 15, supp. 2 (1997).

461 An Executive Summary of the National Business Ethics Survey, conducted by the Ethics Resource Center, is available at: http://www.ethics.org/nbes/nbes2005/index.html

462 O.C. Ferrell, John Fraedrich, and Linda Ferrell, *Business Ethics: Ethical Decision Making and Cases, Sixth Edition* (New York: Houghton Mifflin Company, 2006), 13-14.

Index

Alexander, James 43

Arthur Andersen 10, 29, 30, 37, 38, 42, 45, 52-54, 57-59, 72, 73, 77, 79, 87, 88, 96, 107-109, 113, 117, 119, 122, 124-127, 131, 135-139, 145, 146, 150, 151, 164, 165, 175, 178-183

Avici 89, 97

Azurix 63, 67, 77, 91, 94, 136, 158

Baker, James 33

Bankers Trust 88

Bankruptcy 49, 107, 149, 160-163, 170, 179, 185

Barclay's Bank 53, 151

Bass, Carl 59, 60, 73, 76, 77, 97, 107-109, 113, 131, 137, 180, 182

Baxter, Cliff 75, 94, 95, 113, 162

Bear Stearns 148

Bechtel 40

Belfer, Robert 142

Blockbuster 91, 93, 94, 106

Board of Directors 5, 7, 10, 11, 30, 33, 40-46, 55, 58, 61, 67, 72, 73, 76, 83, 87, 94, 97, 101, 105, 107, 109-111, 117-119, 129, 131, 132, 142, 146, 150, 153, 159, 162-164, 170, 174-176, 181-184, 189, 190

Bonds 11, 13, 30, 138

Bonus 11, 17, 21, 30-34, 37, 41, 47, 54, 57, 58, 60, 63, 74,
    80-83, 94, 98, 109, 119, 131, 146, 153, 154, 157, 158,
    161, 170, 174, 180-182, 188

Bowen, Jack 6, 7

Brazil 63, 64, 74, 94, 139

Bush, George H.W. 14, 18, 30, 32, 101

Bush, George W. 98

Buy, Rick 72, 76

California 39, 48, 49, 62, 89, 90, 94, 97, 101, 105, 107, 112,
    113, 177

CalPERS 39, 52, 53, 150

Carter, Jimmy 14

Causey, Richard 57-60, 71, 75-78, 83-93, 95, 97, 99,
    104-110, 116-121, 124, 126, 129, 131, 133-137, 151,
    163-165, 180-183

Chanos, James 104

Chase Manhattan 36, 76, 148, 161, 183

Chewco 53-55, 66, 80, 85, 96, 115, 132, 147, 150, 151

Canadian Imperial Bank of Commerce (CIBC) 76, 93

Cheney, Dick 101

Ciuaba 74, 75

Citigroup 36, 76, 97, 104, 115, 183

Clinton, Bill 32, 33, 94

Code of Ethics 50, 51, 53-55, 72, 73, 75, 177, 186, 187, 190

Colombia 64, 67

Corporate Raiders 2, 3, 7

Credit Suisse First Boston (CSFB) 70, 73, 76, 86, 148, 183

Dabhol Power Company (DPC) 40-42, 50, 74, 94, 102, 112,
    133, 158

Debt 3-5, 8, 11, 19, 32-35, 41, 42, 50, 53, 57, 60, 63-66, 73, 80, 96, 103, 107, 109, 112, 115, 129, 133, 134, 138, 139, 144, 148, 149, 151, 153, 158-163, 176, 177, 183

Documentation and Retention Policy 137, 138, 145, 146, 153

Dodson, Bill 42, 43

Donaldson, Lufkin & Jenrette 76

Duncan, David 57-60, 72, 73, 77, 87, 88, 96, 107, 108, 126, 131, 135-138, 145, 146, 151, 164, 165, 180-182

Dynegy 149-153, 155, 157-161

Ebarge 79, 88

Electricity 31, 41, 48, 49, 62-64, 68, 79, 89, 90, 94, 95, 97, 101, 105, 107, 112, 157, 177

Emshwiller, John 121, 130, 142, 143

Enron Broadband Services (EBS) 68, 81, 82, 88, 89, 91, 93, 96, 100, 101, 105, 106, 109, 133, 136

Enron Energy Services (EES) 61

Enron Global Power and Pipelines (EPP) 42, 43

Enron Online 78, 161

Enron Wholesale Services 131

Ethical Compliance Audit 186, 189

Ethical Decision-Making Framework 171, 172, 175, 177, 181, 184

ExxonMobile 109, 129

Fastow, Andrew 22-26, 37-39, 41, 42, 48, 50-62, 64-89, 93-99, 103-121, 124, 126-134, 139-151, 155, 158, 162-165, 170, 175-183

Fastow, Lea 52, 178

Fastow Family Foundation 66, 85, 86

Federal Energy Regulatory Commission 112

Federal Power Commission 6

First Union 76

Fleischer, David 111

Florida Gas 6, 31

Fortune 14, 21, 45, 88, 97-99, 104, 105, 109, 110, 161

Frevert, Mark 131

GAAP 54, 57, 73, 78, 80, 135, 182

Gas Bank 14-23, 26-30, 33, 34, 38, 48-50, 56, 64, 100, 174, 175

General Electric 40, 129, 150

Glisan, Ben 57, 75, 84-87, 132, 146, 151

Gramm, Wendy Lee 33

Gray, Rod 42

Grayhawk 83

Great Britain 30-32, 41, 49, 63, 118

Greenspan, Alan 105, 157

Grubman, Richard 110, 144

Harvard 13, 14, 20, 31, 32, 47, 49, 110, 170

Houston Natural Gas (HNG) 3-11, 150

India 39-41, 47, 50, 74, 92, 94, 101, 133

Initial Public Offering (IPO) 42, 67-69, 86, 87, 89, 91, 95, 97

Internal Revenue Service (IRS) 52, 66

InterNorth 7-11, 150, 153

Investment Bankers 16, 27, 28, 36-39, 50, 58, 66, 67, 76, 79, 80, 103-105, 115, 147, 148, 162, 164, 165, 182

Jacobs, Irwin 7, 8, 11

J.P. Morgan 76, 95, 104, 183

JEDI 39, 52-54, 82, 119, 150

Kaminski, Vince 71, 74, 75, 96, 113, 131

Kinder, Richard 17, 34, 42, 45, 46, 56, 60

Kissinger, Henry 33

Kopper, Michael 51-54, 66, 75, 84-87, 115, 132, 151, 177, 178

KPMG 72

Lay, Kenneth 3-23, 31-34, 39, 41, 43-49, 58-63, 66, 72, 77, 81, 88, 91, 94, 97, 98, 101, 102, 104, 110-112, 117-134, 137-147, 150, 153, 155, 157, 159-165, 170, 173-179, 183-185

Lehman Brothers 76

LJMs 68-81, 84-89, 94, 96, 98, 109, 113-115, 126, 130, 132, 138, 142, 143, 146, 149-151, 170

Maharashtra State Electricity Board (MSEB) 40, 94, 101

Mark, Rebecca 32-34, 39-42, 47, 50, 60, 63, 64, 67, 74, 77, 91-94, 119, 176

Mark-to-Market Accounting 26, 28-30, 33, 34, 61, 64, 75, 80, 89, 93, 94, 133, 173-175

Marlin 64, 144

McKinsey & Company 11, 12, 14, 17

McMahon, Jeff 43, 83, 84, 86, 113, 126, 147, 161

McNealy, Scott 82, 83

Merrill Lynch 64, 67, 76, 80, 88, 103, 121, 164, 165, 183

Mordaunt, Kristina 85, 86, 116, 124, 151

Mosbacher, Robert 18, 33

NatWest 70, 85, 86

New York Power Authority 18, 20, 27, 28, 82

Nigeria 77, 79, 88

Nixon, Richard 6

Osprey 66, 103, 104, 116

Pacific Gas & Electric 107

Pai, Lou 95, 112, 142

Pension Plan [401(k)] 140-142, 155

Performance Review Committee (PRC) 56, 128, 176, 189

Porcupine 89

Portland General Electric 49, 50, 90, 107, 133

Prepays 35, 36, 38, 39, 95, 104, 122, 164, 182

PriceWaterhouseCoopers 71

Professional Standards Group (PSG) 77, 97, 107-109, 131, 137, 182

Promigas 64, 67

Put Option 69-72, 85, 87, 89, 107

RADR 50-52, 55, 85, 115, 116

Raptors 86, 89, 96, 107, 109, 119, 124, 131, 137, 151

Reagan Administration 10, 14, 31

Restating Earnings 126, 132, 133, 135-138, 142, 151

Rice, Ken 20, 75, 82, 83, 88, 98, 118

Risk Assessment and Control (RAC) 54, 56, 58, 71

Rythms NetConnections 69-72, 85, 86, 96

Sarbanes-Oxley Act 191

Securities and Exchange Commission (SEC) 28-30, 51, 64, 87, 88, 109, 120, 122, 125, 130, 133-138, 142-146, 149-151, 158, 159, 163, 164, 174, 175, 177-179, 181, 184

Seven Moral Levees 168, 185-191

Short Sellers 104, 110, 111, 113, 142-144

Sierra Pacific 107

Skilling, Jeffrey 11-23, 26-36, 39, 41, 43-50, 53, 54, 56,
   60-78, 81-122, 126, 129-134, 143-147, 151, 159,
   161-165, 170, 173-178, 183, 184

Skillingites 20, 21, 54, 56

Smith, Rebecca 121, 130, 142, 143

Southampton Place 83-87, 116, 124

Special Purpose Entities (SPEs) 24-26, 35-39, 42-44, 53-60,
   63-66, 69-73, 77, 80-88, 93, 96, 97, 102-104, 107,
   113-117, 120, 121, 124, 125, 129, 130, 133, 139, 142-144,
   147, 149-151, 155, 158, 163, 175, 177-179, 182

Standard & Poor's 61, 140, 149, 150

Stock Options 8-10, 20, 21, 33, 43-46, 57, 60, 67, 83, 92,
   93, 97, 98, 112, 115, 119, 122, 131, 153, 157, 163, 170,
   182

Stock Price 3, 36, 39, 43, 45, 50, 58, 61, 62, 65-72, 77-83,
   87, 89, 91, 94, 95, 98, 101-107, 110, 113, 116-118, 121,
   122, 128, 129, 133, 134, 139, 143, 144, 149, 152, 159,
   161, 163, 183, 184

Teesside, England 31, 32, 41, 49, 118

Temple, Nancy 137, 142, 146

Transco 7

UBS Warburg 148

Vietnam War 6

Vinson & Elkins 42, 43, 54, 57, 58, 113, 124, 127, 128,
   131, 182

Walker, Pinkney 6

Wall Street Journal 10, 121, 123, 125, 130, 131, 140, 142,
   143, 146, 147, 151

Waste Management 135, 137

Watkins, Sherron 119, 120, 122, 124, 126-128, 131, 163-165, 178, 179

Watson, Chuck 150

Whalley, Greg 131, 133, 134, 143, 146, 147, 150, 153, 161

Whitewing 66, 67, 103, 116

Wing, John 31, 32, 39

Wyatt, Oscar 4, 5, 7

Printed in the United States
69032LVS00001B/65